A TALE OF
TWO RIVERS

Michael Stephen

DEDICATION

To Pam
who produced our children
for whom this book is written

A TALE OF
TWO RIVERS

Michael St John

The St. John Coat of Arms

BUSHMAIN PUBLISHERS
Aylesbury, England

Bushmain Publishers
10 Mandeville Road
Aylesbury
Buckinghamshire
HP21 8AA

Bushmain Publishers is an imprint of Bushmain
Ltd

First published 1989

Set in Linotron 202 Garamond No 3 by
Dorchester Typesetting Group Ltd, Dorset, and
printed and bound by Biddles Ltd, Surrey.

British Library Cataloguing in Publication Data
St John, Michael, *1915-*
    A tale of two rivers.
    1. Great Britain.   Social life, 1910-1945-
    Biographies
    I. Title
    941.083′092′4

    ISBN 1-85432-002-5

ACKNOWLEDGEMENTS

It is to my children, who by pressing to learn more about the past and their antecedents got me started in the first place, that I must attribute the credit or perchance the blame for this book's existence.

That the resulting random jottings of a few of the more lively episodes got further than a handful of Roneo'ed copies to while away a wet afternoon before consignment to the W.P.B. is due to the help and encouragement of Jeremy and Petra Lewis who in turn passed me on to Bridget Byrne all three offering valuable professional advice, while pushing this idle and belated starter to attempt something more substantial. My grateful thanks to all these kind friends.

Next to receive worthy thanks is Amanda Troubridge who patiently waded through my much corrected script to produce credible type-drafts and forebore to blush at the odd purplish patch.

For the photographs I have selected to enhance these memoirs I have to thank my late Mother's jackdaw instinct that led her to hoard a spectacular collection of old family albums and studio portraits. Also my brother Roger whose editing thereof greatly helped me in making my choice. I must also thank him for bolstering my unstable memory on a number of occasions.

Lastly I come to my erstwhile comrade-in-arms and trusted friend, Johnny Coote, who grabbed me and my script by the lower band and pushed me into the capable hands of Jonathan Newdick, designer, and his sympathetic editor Amanda Gordon-Hall. I regard these three as the midwife and monthly nurses respectively responsible for the birth of this book and I am truly grateful to them for their tender skill and care.

Finally, I humbly express sincere apologies should the more robust episodes concerning what was after all a robust generation, that I have chosen to include in the cause of verisimilitude, offend my readers' sensibilities and thus damage the pleasure that I have sought to provide.

M.B.S^TJ.

Heyshott, 1988

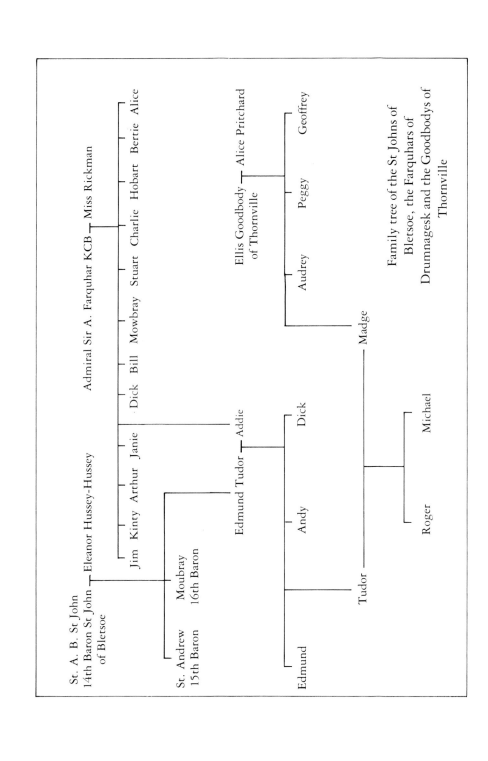

Family tree of the St Johns of Bletsoe, the Farquhars of Drummagesk and the Goodbodys of Thornville

CONTENTS

My parents at Southwood. 1936

INTRODUCTION

In the days with which this book is concerned the postman never failed to deliver a goodly clutch of private letters and no junk mail. Once out of the nursery, family breakfasts were accompanied by the reading aloud of that morning's crop by one parent to the other and vice versa. With servants abounding to take the burden of the household chores off their shoulders, their generation and its predecessor spent their plentiful leisure hours writing copious articulate letters to each other in fine Italianate handwriting, cram-full of diverting gossip and opinions.

So much so that their atmosphere remains fresh in my memory, but alas none of them remain. For this reason both my brother and I at different times during our parents' later years implored them to write down just who was who and what happened where and why in those halcyon days but to no avail. So I am left dredging the depths of recollection in telling as best I can some of the events and people that beset my formative years.

It surprises me that neither my mother or my father took the hint from us as they themselves were prolific correspondents and both wrote salty gems of gossip and comment. The heap of in-coming mail was invariably answered within two or three days, indeed frequently dealt with on the morning of arrival by my mother as soon as she had visited the kitchen to write the orders squeakily on a school slate and cleaned the paraffin lamps with which we lived for many years. Meanwhile my father would likewise be hard at it despatching a steady stream of entertaining letters on House of Commons notepaper from his office overlooking Old Palace Yard.

Now the telephone and easier travel have rendered the art of letter-writing almost moribund and the frantic pace of life in the latter end of the twentieth century leaves little time for it. So as I approach my twilight and before I lose the capacity to do so, I am resolved not be guilty of my parents' sin of omission and to describe for my children, grandchildren and (who knows?) great-grandchildren some of what I can remember of my childhood, adolescence and youth.

Memories are fickle however and should it be that in the course of this book, mine as seems quite likely, proves to have been at fault, I make humble apologies and beg you to accept in a generous frame of mind the best endeavours of an erstwhile sybarite subsiding into his dotage, possessing no claims to fame and endowed with only the none too bounteous share of virtue common to his time and station.

Part I
A THAMESIDE CHILDHOOD

CHAPTER I
Origins

My father, who was a regular soldier, sailed for France with the British Expeditionary Force on 13 August 1914, and I was duly born on 13 May 1915. An example, one might suppose of nature's compensation in time of war to prevent the extinction of the species. On 1 November, during the retreat from Mons, he was so badly wounded that he was not expected to live, so my mother, unintentionally pregnant with me, travelled to Boulogne to be with him.

I thus passively became an overseas traveller at a very early stage in my development, which may partly account for my fondness for 'Abroad' and ending up in the Royal Navy.

I like to register my dislike of the pretentions so frequently paraded by the Celtic and Gaelic fringes of this deceptively termed United Kingdom, by writing English on landing slips, passport applications and suchlike burdens of bureaucracy. In truth I am, like so many other citizens, a comprehensive British mongrel.

My paternal grandpa, Edmund Tudor, was the third son of the Fourteenth Baron St John of Bletsoe, whose unbroken genealogical line recedes into the mists of French and English pre-history. I have heard them rudely described as the longest line of undischarged bankrupts in England. Being founder's kin he went from Harrow to St John's College, Cambridge, founded by our ancestor Lady Margaret Beaufort, whence in 1874 he followed the customary destiny of third sons by being ordained

Limerick 1910. My parents en route for their Honeymoon, saying good-bye to the employees of J. Bannatyne's flour mills

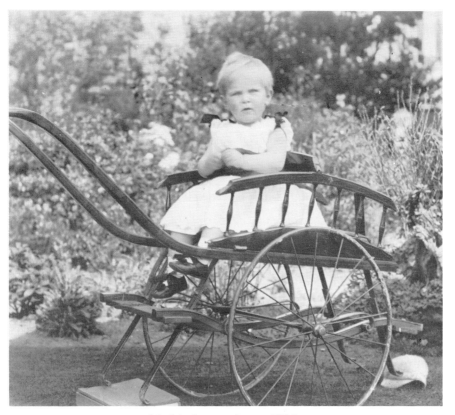

My Mother aged one. 1890

an anglican priest by the Bishop of Peterborough. He not surprisingly became installed as Rector of Bletsoe in Bedfordshire, whence he moved in 1876 to the Episcopal parish of Christ Church Kincardine-O-Neil, and married in 1877 my Scottish grandmother, Adeline, third daughter of Admiral Sir Arthur Farquhar KCB of Drumnagesk, Aberdeenshire. They had four sons in the rapid succession of Victorians: Edmund; my father, Tudor; Andy and Dick; but when my father was just past his fifth birthday, my grandfather was killed fielding unwisely at silly mid-on in a game of extremely bucolic cricket on a more than picturesque pitch.

So it was that my father and his brothers were brought up fairly wild by their widowed mother at her capacious Deeside home, Drumnagesk, in the bosom of the Clan Farquhar where she had taken over as Châtelaine to the old Admiral following Lady Farquhar's demise.

Tales of their formative years are many; their wildness often escaping from the strictures of the heavy Victorian morality of the parson's widow. Of such strictures the following is a startling example. Having been seriously hit in the orchestra while playing cricket at the age of nine, evidently no better than Grandpa at the game, my father was laid up with a thing the size of a football which eventually had to be removed. Before this was accomplished, my grandmother found him innocently showing the phenomenon to the friendly Scots housemaid, whom she promptly sacked, and confiscated the new bible he had recently won at Sunday School 'for reciting the (Nth) Chapter of the (Whatever) word-perfectly'. The Bible still exists with the following fearful endictment in my grandmother's handwriting below the above citation: 'Confiscated for immoral conduct' and the date. Truly it may be said of those days: to the Puritan all things are impure.

My father went first with his younger brothers, my uncles Andy and Dick, to the RNC Britannia, but as he had grown up with a stammer that failed to respond to treatment Their Lordships decided he was unfit for the Senior Service before he even became seaborne. After filling in time at Aberdeen University he was eventually commissioned into the Royal Northumberland Fusiliers, The 'Fighting Fifth', with which regiment he in due course found himself pleasantly garrisoned in Limerick shortly after the turn of the century.

Aunt Audrey and my Mother. 1893

Thornville, Limerick before Ellis Goodbody created his garden

Military duties were undemanding and largely concerned with riding to hounds (not he though, for horses have never been partial to St Johns), fishing (at which he excelled), shooting and a full and uninhibited social life, in the midst of which he met and married Madeleine (always Madge), the eldest of the three daughters of Ellis Goodbody of Thornville. Ellis was the prosperous head of the family flour-milling business; a descendant of one of Cromwell's Irish quakers (his mother, incidentally was a sister of the Ellis brothers who founded and built the Midland Railway). He had married Alice Pritchard from North Wales.

So there you have it: English St Johns, Scottish Farquhars on one side and Irish Goodbodys with Welsh Pritchards on the other – comprehensively a citizen of the then United Kingdom but, as a St John, English.

Sadly Ellis Goodbody died of pneumonia in 1915 aged only 56, shortly before I was born, so I never knew either of my grandfathers. Now that I am one myself I find this a source of regret. From all that I have gleaned about them they were very different characters, each in his way someone commanding much respect and affection. Edmund St John a scholarly and very sporting parson; and Ellis Goodbody a leading figure in the business and social life of the south west of Ireland. The latter's good looks and charm show clearly in the many photographs he took or organised so well. I have a delightful faded example of him playing Cat's Cradle with his little son Geoffrey. It is clear that my mother, his first-born, was his favourite until many years later when his son Geoffrey was born; and equally evident to me from her many recollections that she adored her father. It must have been a terrible blow to her when he died just as when I, unintended, was on the way and her husband so badly wounded that she could not expect him to survive; events that I shall describe later. She was 26 at the time and clearly a very brave and resilient woman to have come through all that in one piece.

She has described vividly to me how versatile and forward-looking Ellis Goodbody was. He was the first to acquire a motor car in that part of Ireland; a monumental open touring car in which he drove many miles around the West, usually with his eldest child, Madge, to accompany

My parents on their wedding day, 10th March 1910. From left to right: Ellis Goodbody, Alice Goodbody, my parents, The Rev. A. Noyse, Adeline St John and Edmond St John

The Goodbody's car at Thornville. 1908. My parents and Grandfather in the
back seat. Geoffrey "driving", Peggy in front seat. My Grandmother and
Audrey in the porch. Hanly the Chauffeur/Groom

him. It was her duty to clear the road of the panic-stricken local traffic. The donkeys or ponies never wavered in the face of this smelly and noisy phenomenon and stood rooted to the centre of the road while the occupants fled every which way into the adjoining bogs. So Madge disembarked, led the ass-cart/side-car past the motor and, leaving it to await its craven owners, regained the front seat and they were off again to the next encounter.

He was also a keen and green-fingered gardener who introduced the first herbaceous border into south west Ireland, which rapidly acquired widespread fame. This he had to do in the face of strong native radical views and the obdurate obstinacy of Keegan, the Thornville head gardener. It was, I gather, an attenuated war of attrition exhibiting the utmost resolve and patience on my grandfather's part and it ended in triumph with Keegan's bedding-out propensities, so dear and all-absorbing to his breed, being confined to the large circular bed in the centre of the gravel sweep before the front door. A serious and lengthy meeting between Ellis and Keegan took place once a year prior to sending off the seedsmens' orders – watched always by Madge who herself became a skillful gardener. She related how Keegan's recital of his complicated plan for the layout always ended ". . . and then, Sor, I t'ort we'ed boind it aul with a bit of lobayliar!" With which Grandpa, who hadn't been paying much attention, of course agreed.

To photography, motoring and gardening, Ellis added a keen appreciation of music, singing all Percy French's splendid ditties with a pleasing baritone and ensuring that his daughters had the best teachers, my mother of the violin and Audrey the piano. My mother finished at the Paris Conservatoire from which she was occasionally able to join the Opéra's second violins, thus hearing de Reske, Melba and many others from the orchestra pit. She told of how de Reske, who loathed Nellie Melba, on one occasion put a large chamberpot under the bed on which she lay dying in Act III of Bohème, making great play of avoiding kicking it, to the Parisian audience's huge delight and the detriment of Melba's performance.

Life for regular officers in smart regiments such as the Fifth was not, as I have mentioned, very demanding in those halcyon Edwardian days

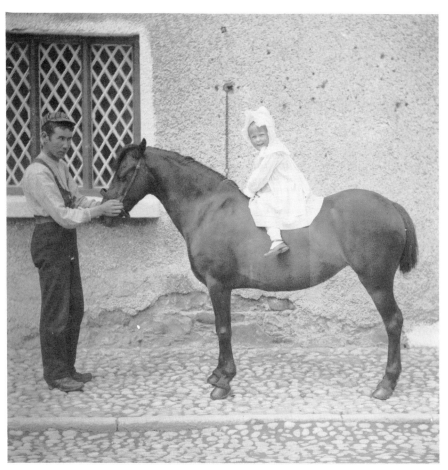

My Mother at Thornville. 1893

Granny Goodbody with Audrey and my Mother. 1891

Granny St John with her four sons, Dick, Andy, Edmund and Tudor. c. 1905

My Mother, 1909

and unusually Ireland at that time was more or less free of troubles – on the surface anyway. It seems to have been balls, picnics and parties all the way and there was a plentiful supply of gorgeous girls among the Frenchs, Gatacres, Kennedys and many other western Irish families, with the Goodbody girls very much in the swim: Madge the spun-gold blonde; Audrey the blue-eyed brunette and Peggy a chocolate-box nymph in those days. The flirting and goings-on between these spirited beauties and the garrison was aptly summed up by old Mrs Kennedy once declaring "The shtair-carpets is worn out with the thrampling of the cavalry".

My parents were married after a long engagement once my mother was 21 in 1910. They had a vast wedding in Limerick Cathedral attended

My Great Grandmother, Lady St John

My Great Grandfather, Lord St John of Bletsoe

by many people from Counties Clare, Limerick, Kerry and Cork, plus much of the Dublin 'Quality' and a host of my father's relations. There was also one uninvited guest in the person of Edith Somerville's wild youngest brother Aylmer, who had been purposely excluded from the Somerville family's invitation because of his highly uncertain behaviour (he is considered to be largely the model for the notorious Flurry Knox in the Somerville and Ross stories). But come he did, without a wedding garment and reduced the wedding group to chaos with his antics.

According to custom, my father as a newly-wed officer was appointed Garrison Adjutant at the regiment's depot in Newcastle, an undemanding post that left ample opportunity for the happy couple to settle down together. This my parents did in Hexham where in the following year my elder and only brother Roger was duly born. As far as I know they continued to enjoy a pretty free and untramelled life in Geordieland for the next few years, in fact the army contrived to lose my father on indefinite leave for over two years. They made many friends up there who I later came to know.

Eventually, of course, all this was to change. By the beginning of 1914 my father was back with the regiment as a Company Commander garrisoned at Dover Castle. By the time war was becoming inevitable, they had moved to Victoria Barracks in Southsea and my parents, with Roger and his Irish nanny, into a rented house in Palmerston Road.

It was thence the Fifth departed, via Southampton and Le Havre, for the Belgian front and the infamous retreat from Mons. So was I born into a civilisation facing what was to prove possibly the greatest upheaval since Attila the Hun.

My St John Grandparents

My newly-wed parents on Birse Loch, 1910

Wedding Guests at Thornville, 10th March 1910

Edmund and Tudor St John. 1882

My Father as Subaltern in the Fifth Fusiliers

CHAPTER II
War and peace

My father's regiment moved straight up to the Belgian front on arrival in Le Havre and soon became all too hotly engaged in rearguard actions during the retreat from Mons. By October they were entrenching themselves about eight miles south of Ypres and it was on 1 November that my father was caught in machine-gun fire while crossing a turnip field near Wytschacht to visit one of his forward outposts. He later wrote a diary of all these events as well as his subsequent rescue and miraculous recovery. One of the bullets had traversed from beneath his left shoulder upwards across his chest after he had fallen on his face. It ended in his trachea, missing heart and lungs en route. He was full of holes and breathing through one in his neck which saved his life but rendered him unable to speak. While laying on a stretcher in a casualty-clearing station (only those expected to live were moved onto paliasses) a medical orderly went through his pockets and relieved him of his watch and some gold sovereigns. He claimed that the wave of frustrated rage that swept through him at being unable to tell anyone what had happened probably kept him alive until he got to Boulogne and eventually, in December 1914, onto a Hospital Ship.

Once my pregnant mother had got herself to Boulogne in response to telegrams she was helped by my Great-Uncle Bertie Farquhar (of whom more later), who was driving ambulances there and who had managed to find my father. She remained with my father until he was shipped back to Southampton and thence by train to The Honourable Mrs Burns's hospital in Torquay. It was here that eventually a doctor saved his life after many alarms by performing an emergency low tracheotomy without an anaesthetic, during which he managed to cough out an abcess the size of two fists that was by then suffocating him. Thereafter he started slowly to recover and was for many months at Sister Agnes's, in Grosvenor Gardens, undergoing a lengthy series of major operations. He was a big man, a hefty six feet, but when I was born the following May he weighed only seven stone.

My St John grandmother had moved south to look after my pregnant mother and be in on the action, renting 11 Bolton Gardens where I first saw the light of day. I was soon displayed with much pride to my still pretty sick father who said, "I told you Madge, not to go to the zoo while you were pregnant", for which he got a round telling off from Sister Agnes who had taken us to see him.

Sister Agnes was, of course, a thorough-going old snob but a most effective one, cajoling the high and mighty from the Monarch downwards to support her splendid efforts for serving officers. It was the custom during the Great War for her to take parties of convalescing wounded officers, weather permitting, to the gardens of Buckingham Palace for tea with King George V and Queen Mary. They went in through the gate by the traffic lights at the bottom of Grosvenor Place. One day my father was wheeled in on a chair and lined up with the others to be presented. Wounded officers wore civilian clothes in 1915 – the inevitable Marlborough jacket and bowler hat – and as the King and Queen came down the line shaking hands, my father, with difficulty, got himself standing up with the aid of two sticks and put his bowler on the seat behind him to make it easier to shake the Royal hands. Seeing how frail he was, the King told him to sit down and my father, in his relief, forgot the hat and started to subside gratefully into his wheelchair. Queen Mary, close behind the King, spotted the impending disaster and leapt forward with her rapier-like parasol to knock the bowler out of harm's way, but succeeded in impaling it like a brochette and waving it aloft to everyone's huge delight, King George V's in particular.

During my father's long and often difficult convalescence I was posted off to Granny Goodbody in Limerick, my mother being totally involved in the nursing of him while the Irish nanny took care of four-year old Roger. Being tubed following the tracheotomy, my father used to wear a specially designed cravat with a hole through which the inner filter tube protruded looking like a stock-pin. It was jointed, like a tiny string of sausages, and slipped through the outer tube which resembled an old fashioned curved motor horn and led like a fair-lead through his neck below the larynx into his windpipe at a 90 degree bend. The inner filter had to be changed regularly; a very delicate and painful process that took a long time to achieve. I tell you this because on the last occasion he wore uniform (and was thus cravatted) for the Fifth Fusiliers' Armistice celebrations in Newcastle, he arrived by train into a jostling and excitable melée at the station and suddenly found difficulty breathing. The filter tube that took so long and with such pain to change was gone, without his feeling a twinge. Such is the speed and skill of the professional pickpocket, but this chap must have been sorely puzzled by his loot! My father always carried a spare and so survived, but the incident evidently caused quite a stir and 26 years later we discovered that by chance my wife Pam's Uncle Sam and Aunt Alfhild Guinness were there and remembered every detail. They were fascinated to learn that the officer concerned was the man who eventually became their niece's father-in-law.

My father, having survived his wounds after long hospital treatment and many major operations, had been invalided out of the army as 100% disabled with no pension and only a 'wound gratuity' – £20 a hole or something equally ludicrous. He was lucky enough to be selected, as a regular soldier with a family of two boys, as the object of a group of philanthropists, headed by Lord Wittenham, who secured him a job as HM Deliverer of The Vote on the Speaker's staff in the House of Commons and provided the Old Mill House on his estate at Benson beside the Thames above Wallingford to go with it.

When my parents were safely settled there in 1916 and my father had started his light duties at the House of Commons, I was returned to the bosom of my family and a happy bosom it was despite our somewhat straitened circumstances. In those days even penniless ex-soldiers kept a bevy of domestic servants and we had cook, kitchen-maid (a junior drudge always much put upon), housemaid and parlourmaid. We also had a full-time gardener from the village and, of course, our nanny – all on my father's salary of £400 a year as Head of the Vote Office plus very little else.

Roger and I were mostly confined to our nursery up the back stairs behind the green-baize door as was customary for upper middle-class children then, so we were closer to the domestics than to our parents. One of my earliest recollections is of Maggie, the catholic Irish cook, who with Minnie the likewise nanny hung the kitchen with bloody allegorical oleographs of the Sacred Heart and sundry martyrs being eviscerated, broken on wheels, raped or used for target practice. These filled me with fascinated horror and a goodly bunch of infant misapprehensions. Minnie didn't last long as she was found to be bullying Roger, who like his father had developed a stammer. She was succeeded by Letty Hellyer, whom we adored. A dark blue-eyed, buxom person from Gomshall with a musical Surrey voice – I later identified Peggotty with her when I came to read *David Copperfield*. Letty stayed with us until I was packed off to join Roger at Ashdown House prep-school, just before my eighth birthday in 1923. Long after that we continued to keep in touch with her and to meet her for walks in Kensington Gardens with her new charges whenever we were in London, usually on the way to or from school.

For many years, till she got married, the housemaid was a local girl called Florence, another good friend to spoilt little boys. She went to live in neighbouring Shillingford where she took in laundry including my mother's massive trousseau of Irish linen and all the family's smalls. It was years before we were exposed to the depredations of a steam laundry, and even then huge hampers of washing were sent parcel post to Pullars of Perth, then the acknowledged Rolls Royce of the laundry trade.

Maggie disappeared back to the bogs soon after Minnie's departure and was replaced by our invaluable family friend and superb cook, Mary Norris from nearby Wallingford. She remained with my parents until they retired to Scotland in 1941 and we all kept in touch with her, wherever in the world we might be, until her death in the '50s. Dear old Norris – how lucky we were to have her with us and for so long. She was completely devoted to us, severally and collectively, and such loyalty, coupled with a grand sense of humour and great skill in feeding us royally was a rare and precious part of our lives during my boyhood. She was a frail, sharp-featured little person with her thin, mousey hair parted in the centre into wide wings that swept past her ears and ended in a well-rivetted bun on top. Later, after we had moved to Henley, she loved to go to the WI whist drives to which we ferried her. She always came back with a prize which caused Roger and me unkindly to wonder about her ethics at the card table! Needless to say birthdays were unfailingly marked by a cake appropriate to the individual – in my case coffee – and in due course goodies were regularly despatched to us at school. Roger and I, when at home, started each day by visiting the kitchen on instructions to bid good-morning and enquire after her health. In later years this might lead to a grisly account of her legs that 'were weeping badly' or some such that was hard to bear on top of a hefty breakfast.

The gardener at the Old Mill House was Mr Harris, who lived in a very pretty cottage in Benson. He was an elderly scrawny man with a red and wrinkled weather-beaten face and no teeth. He had one of those fascinating Adam's apples that stick out like miniature pyramids and jerk up and down when their possessor swallows. He was invariably tricked out in curled up hobnail boots, a green baize apron and a bowler hat. I often contrived to visit the kitchen when he came in for his elevenses and gaze in wonderment at that madly jumping Adam's apple and incomprehension as to how he managed to consume his bun or wad without teeth.

Benson Church is blessed with a fine peal of eight bells and Mr Harris was leader of the bell-ringers, a position of quite some importance in the village. Those bells are another nostalgic childhood memory; they were in frequent melodious use and their distant sound would come softly floating across the flat fields of the Thames Valley, through the open window of my night nursery and lull me to sleep. The ringers always performed before and after matins and I loved to watch them through the west door which led into the square bell-tower. When I was a little older I was allowed to stay up at home to hear them ring the old year out and the new year in.

My mother had inherited her father's skill and zeal as a gardener and spent much of her time producing, with old Harris's patient help, a beautiful garden matching the early eighteenth century house which came to be much admired. The house itself was such a perfect example of Queen Anne's era that the Wittenhams refused to have it wired for electricity or plumbed for central heating, so we lived with paraffin lamps, candles and coal fires. My mother personally cleaned, filled and trimmed all the lamps herself every morning, with the result that we never smelt paraffin or suffered sudden belchings of black smoke, but enjoyed soft lambent light in winter evenings and spotless brass lamps to take to bed.

We had a grandfather clock in the hall, the weights of which had, with much noisy grinding of chains, to be pulled up every 24 hours. This my mother regularly did on her way to bed (and continued to do till shortly before she died aged 93). This sound was our signal to blow out our lamps and quickly assume deep sleep before she came to tuck us up – no good of course, because she was always alerted by the lamp's red-hot chimney and we would get a beefy back-hander as well as a kiss.

The house stood behind a clipped hedge and railings on the lane running beside the Thames from Benson to Preston Crowmarsh. Its classic Queen Anne façade of pitched roof topping five first floor sash windows and two pairs of taller ones flanking the front door at ground level, was entirely covered by wistaria, so that only in wintertime could you fully appreciate the mellow old brickwork. We looked over the lane to a water-meadow split by the mill-stream; itself split by an island giving house-room to a vast weeping willow. Beyond flowed the Thames, invisible between steep, willow-dotted banks and then the further fields sloped gently up to a low treeless horizon – over which in the distance rose the local landmark of the Wittenham Clumps. In those pre-chemical, organic days the summer meadows were alight with wild flowers and teeming with many butterflies and insects, while the reeds and irises beside the river were iridescent with flashing, many-coloured dragonflies.

Our gardens ran back from the house towards more flat fields (now the RAF airfield), about one and a half acres of kitchen and flower gardens, a tennis court and an overgrown orchard. Beyond, through a wicket gate in a line of lofty, rook-inhabited elms, lay our Granny Goodbody's house, Greenhayes, to which she had moved after the 1916 rebellion. She was the best sort of spoiling granny that anyone could wish for. Treats at tea-time meant a generous spoonful of black cherry jam lurking unseen at the bottom of one's mug of milk to assure its consumption, wonderful birthday and Christmas presents, a never-failing sanctuary for wayward children when in doubtless well-earned disgrace. She was a handsome, smallish person, always very neat in smart black and white clothes; a devout Anglo-Catholic who never missed church, as well as a confirmed patriot who stood whenever the national anthem was played on the wireless. Her maiden sister, our Great-Aunt Marg, was often staying with her at Greenhayes, another sweet and affectionate person of remarkable but inoffensive ugliness, who adored all children and spoiled us rotten.

These two sisters were superb knitters and provided all their relations, including us, with beautiful, fully-fashioned golf stockings all with differently patterned tops, plus socks and pullovers of every imaginable stitch. Both of them continued this welcome labour of love almost to the day they died and I must record our undying gratitude.

So you see, Greenhayes was a very noticeable bonus in our childhood days at Benson.

We had no car till I was 15, an enforced economy, but some time earlier than that Granny, under strong family pressure, acquired a two-seater Wolseley which my mother learned adequately to drive, often with us boys wrapped up in the unsheltered dickey. Life was otherwise sustained by the Oxford bus from Benson, the train to Reading from nearby Wallingford, or Mr Munday and his ancient, odiferous, rattling Renault taxi which ferried us to the Wallingford spur of the GWR and to dances and parties.

He invariably took my father to the station en route for the House of Commons. This was not every day as the latter spent the middle of the week with Aunt Carrie Rickman, who lived in some style at 39 Cadogan Place and kept a chauffeur-driven Rolls and a bevy of old retainers. She was in fact the widow of my Great-Great-Uncle Stuart Rickman, the much younger brother of Lady Farquhar the old Admiral's wife. Aunt Carrie was very much part of our life, providing a luxurious London base for pantomimes-cum-staging-post en route to and from school. She was a frequent visitor to the Old Mill House and later to Southwood, our house near Henley, as well as a regular summer visitor to Deeside, where, as I shall later relate, we mostly spent our summer holidays. Aunt Carrie was a Buchanan and very proud of her Scottish nationality. I remember well the Monday departures for in addition to his attaché-case my father was burdened with a shallow wicker basket full of flowers from the garden carefully packed by my mother for Aunt Carrie. Even in winter there were flowers from the capacious greenhouse. Male chauvinism being still rampant, my mother always helped him on with his overcoat, handing him his umbrella and bowler and giving him a final brush-down before kissing him goodbye.

We were a very spoilt family in those days, but in fairness I think deservedly so. My father was widely acclaimed as a hero, not only because he was among the first casualties of that ghastly war before people became numbed by the endless lists of the dead and wounded on the Somme, but all the more so for having been counted as dead and fighting through such severe wounding to be one of the first human beings to be tubed like a horse. To this must be added the widespread sympathy and admiration inspired by my then 26-year-old mother's courage, who in one year had lost a much loved father, fled to her supposedly dying husband in France, mistakenly pregnant, and thereafter nursed my father with an inspiring devotion that was to continue for the rest of his 84 years. All this with cheerfulness and good humour from them both and not a jot of self-pity.

And so here is the pensionless war hero and his young family, happily and well, if simply, found in the as yet unspoilt open spaces of the upper Thames Valley, in a beautiful Queen Anne house, with kind and devoted Granny Goodbody next door at Greenhayes and equally kind and devoted Great-Great-Aunt Carrie supporting us in London. No car, but hosts of friends and relations, including most importantly our St John grandmother, exchanging the long visits fashionable in those days and tended by loyal and friendly domestic servants.

For me as for many it was to be memories of endless sunlit days or crisp frosty winters with the thrill of many credulous Christmases, all of which I will endeavour to describe in my next chapter.

My Mother and me aged six at The Old Mill House. 1921

CHAPTER III

Childhood at Benson

Our nursery was on the first floor of an addition to the west side of the house, set well back from the original Queen Anne façade. Beneath was the kitchen which kept it cosy, and in winter we had a coal fire encased in the usual nursery fireguard hooked to the wall and perpetually festooned with airing combinations, pyjamas and socks. The floor was covered in dark sage-green cork flooring with two or three washable rugs here and there and we had a fine deal table for meals (and later on lessons) in front of a bow-window, that we often adapted as a mini theatre in order to give agonising theatrical performances to an amazed and patient household. Otherwise, except for a few chairs, a chest-of-drawers and a hideous green-marbled painted sideboard for a toy-cupboard, it was left conveniently unencumbered for our activities.

I can remember one day trying to hide under the table during a game with Roger and pulling the cloth down to the floor, forgetting in the frantic excitement of his simulated stealthy approach of a hungry leopard, that it was laid for tea, luckily sans scalding pot. Roger was bombarded with breaking crockery and for me instant supperless bed ensued. I also recollect seizing and brandishing the breadknife in another like frissante encounter and almost having his thumb off. Luckily Lady Wittenham was having tea below on that occasion and her chauffeur was able to rush him to the surgery in Wallingford so he still has two thumbs. I suppose I was then three or four years old and Roger seven or eight. It must have been shortly after 1918 because my earliest memory is of a large union jack being hoisted over the front door on a pole for the Armistice, not that I was remotely aware of the war other than as a tiresome mystery that curtailed my supply of sweets, but it seemed such a very funny thing to do.

It was about then that my parents took Roger to see Mr Harmer my father's ENT consultant about his stammer which resulted in endless speech therapy for us both and lying flat for 20 minutes each day on the hearth-rug with a book balanced on our chests, which we had to keep unmoved while deep-breathing. I was included in this treatment presumably as a precaution and to keep Roger company. Anyway, I never had a stammer and Roger gradually outgrew his — I can hear now our dreary lentissimo litany, "Conquering Kings their Titles Take" and other like tongue twisters.

You can imagine that, as the two of us grew up together, I became wholly dependent in all our games on the leadership of my near-four years older and worshipped only brother so that when, with me five and he nine years old, he was whisked off to prep-school, I was utterly undone. I wept copiously for days and found myself quite unable to play by myself for many weeks after his harrowing departure (he, poor chap, was always very homesick).

Although able to be moderately active six years after his wounding, my father was still whispering with his tube in place. But then one day my mother suggested that I started asking God in my prayers to let Daddy speak — not again, mind you, for I had only ever heard him whisper. This I duly did and back he came one day sans tube and doing so. Although it was an unforgettable moment, I can't recollect that I related this apparent miracle directly to my orisons or became convinced of the efficacy of prayer. So the ethics of my mother's deception, while causing me some puzzling thought in later life, did no conscious harm.

Our country walks, at first in a pram and later on the hoof, are still a vivid memory; beside the brook, along the road to the watercress beds at ancient Ewelme; round the many footpaths that wound through the wide flat fields, where we often watched them tilling, a steel hawser towing the plough back and forth between two steam traction engines. In summer, it would be through the wicket gate across our road past the mill and over the dangerous wooden gangways of the weir with only a single handrail and through the shut gates of Benson Lock to the farther meadows. Another sortie took us up the Oxford road to Shillingford, past Haines' Wharf where we got our eggs, to see Florence, the ci-devant housemaid. We collected the eggs in a shallow, circular basket with a hoop handle and it was one of our favourite dares, invoking Letty's wrath, to whirl it round over one's head as if heaving the lead – there was the occasional disaster, of course, and swift retribution, which made it all the more fun. When I was quite small I used to enjoy teasing Mrs Haines' chickens, until I got chased off by an angry cockerel one day, which scared me stiff and caused much merriment for Mrs Haines and Letty.

Our clothes would seem odd nowadays. There were gaiters for winter walks, with dozens of buttons up the outside reaching well above the knees – how that button hook could pinch if carelessly wielded by an impatient Letty running late. We always wore combinations till we were kitted out for boarding school, a strange bodice made of some flannelly stuff that impractically buttoned up the back and, until about age five, a short brown holland smock with matching pants beneath for everyday. For best, a white belted linen tunic and shorts. For parties and presentations to important guests we suffered till we were six or so in crêpe-de-chine – usually eau-de-nil – which I hated.

I remember well that I was in my white linen outfit during a tea-party at Greenhayes when Aunt Marg in a game of hide-and-seek so frightened me by creeping towards me hiding behind but clearly visible through a bush that I conclusively wet myself and burst into terrified tears. Kind Aunt Marg swiftly got me home and changed before wrath could descend.

There are some deathless studio photographs of me so garbed taken in Reading by a man with a considerable reputation at the time. I remember my new shoes were pinching and I was in a foul temper.

Lessons started for me when I was three years old as by then Roger had already completed two years voyage into the realms of the three Rs

Me and Roger, The Old Mill House.
1917. I am modelling my smock

Wolseley – our first car

with our governess Hilda (at that time 'Miss' to us) Field, spinster daughter of the venerable white-bearded vicar of Benson. It was the only way of keeping me quiet now that the nursery had become the schoolroom.

Hilda Field, it was clear, would always be a spinster, but I don't suppose this caused her a moment's regret: pale, kind and clever, she had two outstanding and contrasting characteristics: a beautiful soft, contralto speaking voice and appalling halitosis. *Reading Without Tears, Pot-hooks* and *Two-Times-Table* are to me forever evocative of bad breath. I was always lazy and was made to do extra reading under severe and often painful conditions with my father flipping a short length of string with a knot on its end across my fat legs as I sat on his knee whenever I made a mistake – hardly Montessori methods, but I came to no lasting harm and could read adequately before I was five.

Miss Field stayed on as governess till I went to Ashdown, but later when by myself, I used to walk the footpaths for about a mile to join her for lessons in the vicarage. On several occasions I was ambushed en route by gangs of village boys whose courage luckily melted in the face of my frail façade of bravado that thinly covered inward terror. Hilda was, and afterwards remained, a firm family friend and as with Letty we never missed a chance to look her up and I am glad to say she often came to stay with us.

Soon Roger was old enough for model railways and naturally I was included in the new enthusiasm, so that Christmases and birthdays were wholly devoted to increasing our stock till we had a formidable array from Basset-Lowke and Hornby with which we were forever altering our layouts on the nursery floor. Once in the summer we took it all out to the vast rubbish heap in the orchard and created a marvellous scenic railway with tunnels, bridges and embankments all over my mother's extensive well-rotted compost heap. This in time inspired us, when we had been left alone one late-autumn day in the post-Letty era, to carry some of this compost into the nursery to add realism to our permanent way. There was a well heaped-up coal fire going which we found became too hot, so Roger got a basin of water and threw it on the red-hot coals with, of course, utterly disastrous consequences. Very luckily neither of us was scalded by the resulting explosion of super-heated steam but the whole room was saturated and the floor became a sea of rich mud – Ye Gods, the row that broke when our tired parents got back from Newbury Races whence they had struggled by train, changing twice each way, and I suspect having lost money to boot for my father had been a reckless gambler in his salad days.

After trains the salient memory is of the indescribable thrill of suddenly getting away solo on my first bike. The speed, the rushing air, the sense of freedom. Thereafter we were pedalling for miles around and almost daily did the messages for my mother in Wallingford, a beautiful and historic riverside town, quite unspoilt in those days and possessing one of the finest of Thames bridges with redundant toll-house at its centre. I remember Mr Crudgington, the fishmonger, looking exactly like the cod on his slab under his boater; Mr Davies, the antiques dealer in his Georgian house, with whom my mother was forever driving bargains; the town drapers, a perfectly-preserved relic of the late Victorian/Edwardian era with the appropriate and unforgettable name of Field, Hawkins and Ponking and complete with broad counters, yardsticks, high bent-wood chairs for customers and overhead railways to take your invoice and cash inside a hollow wooden ball to the somewhat frightening cashier, resembling a predatory spider at the centre of the converging rails. After tearing the balls apart, she despatched them with a sharp tug on a sort of lavatory chain back whence they came with your change and receipt. I never saw her, or her sisters in the similarly equipped Heelas of Reading, ever send a ball off on the wrong line, despite extended waiting in eager anticipation. The drapers faced across the Market Place on to the inevitable arcaded Corn Exchange forming the gently busy heart of the town.

While I was still quite small, our summers were often concerned with trips on the river. Granny had a punt at Haines' Wharf, many of our friends had more exciting skiffs and the old Burkitts even had an electric canoe which was a rare, but special thrill. But what I liked best were the steamers, with their hot oil and steam smells rising from the engine-room skylights, the brass funnels that had to be pulled down aft by a rope to pass under bridges, the clanging of the bridge telegraphs and

Cadet St John. The Old Mill House. 1929

The Old Mill House, Benson

the piercing siren which always caught you unawares. The beauties of the upper reaches of the Thames need no extolling, and they were free of motor-launches and houseboats in my childhood, but I must confess it was the strawberries and cream for tea at Day's Lock that stands out like a beacon, rather than the many charms of the slowly moving landscape, with the rushes bending in our wake.

Another delight of those early years were the regular visits to the Old Mill House side gate of an entrancing barrel-organ drawn by a donkey wearing a tarpaulin rug painted with the Union Jack and emblazoned 'RSPCA'. The proprietor of the equippage was our close friend for he always let us turn the handle and change the tune when we went down from the nursery to put our pennies in both the donkey's box and his hat. He closely resembled Edith Somerville's drawings of the notorious Slipper in *The Experiences of an Irish RM*. Then his visits ceased all of a sudden and I never discovered why but we sorely missed him. I suppose he must have died.

When I was about nine or ten, we were joined by our first cousin, Desmond Fitzgerald, Audrey's son. She and her husband Otho had settled in Kenya, so Desmond came to live mostly with his Aunt Madge and Uncle Tudor while he attended boarding school with me at Ashdown before going on to Wellington. For me this was a great boon as I was no longer the youngest and had someone to whom in turn I could pass on the chores and burdens of the average family household: "Be an angel . . ." was the unfailing opening gambit and Desmond was soon beatified. However, his presence was not all in my favour since he turned out to be annoyingly clever and diligent and I had to work hard to maintain a respectable distance ahead of him in our struggle up the slopes of Academe.

It was still possible in those well-staffed days for people to pay lengthy visits to each other and for the Big Houses to entertain a procession of house-parties for shooting, fishing or the main events of the social season both in England and the north. We were no exception to this way of life, with the spare room at home being more often occupied than empty as it received a regular procession of old friends and relatives. Which brings me to our St John granny, known always to us as Gan-Gan (to distinguish her from Granny Goodbody) and to the World as Aunt Addie.

She made a regular yearly progress to the south from her home at Aboyne on Deeside starting with a month at the Old Mill House. Her advent was presaged by the arrival per Passenger's Luggage in Advance (PLA) of a vast wicker trunk with a domed lid which was covered in black canvas and marked The Hon Mrs E T St John in huge white painted letters. This was accompanied by her inseparable companion, a bicycle of some age and consequence. Green and gold with ivory handles, Melton cloth saddle-cover, silk-thread guards over the rear wheel to protect trailing (usually Farquhar Tartan) skirts, it came standing majestically in a fantastic custom-built erection of rattan and bamboo that closely resembled a section of the Forth Railway Bridge. To a small boy it seemed to reach almost to the sky and its gleaming splendour struck awe into the breast. Gan-Gan never possessed a car, having ridden this same stately bone-shaker great distances all her life and continuing so to do until she was 83 when to her fury, after a mild heart attack, my Uncle Andy put it out of bounds. This advance consignment was duly unpacked ready for its owner; my mother once complaining in my hearing that inter alia the trunk contained over 20 assorted pairs of footwear.

Our lack of grandfathers was certainly offset by our two devoted, diverse and delightful grandmothers, entirely different from each other and entirely to be loved and spoiled by. Gan-Gan had inherited the fine silver-haired distinction of the Farquhars with kind warm brown eyes and a peerless complexion. A slim upright figure dressed always in a tartan skirt, except when going to London, and hung about with many gold chains, fob-watches, beads and a pair of pince-nez on a black ribbon. She used to reduce me to helpless hysterical laughter with those pince-nez by pretending to sneeze "A-*tish*-ooh" and off they would fly. She loved to read aloud to us which she did beautifully but alas usually from sickly, 'improving' and maudlin Victorian children's books such as *Mary's Meadow, Jackanapes, Misunderstood* or *Little Lord Fauntleroy*. Over these horrors she would weep copiously as she read of the deprivations, drudgery and early deaths from consumption which always ended –

unconvincingly to me – in a halo of light, safe in the arms of Jesus (so who would they play with? I wondered). However, the sneezing gambit followed by the crash of specs among the beads and other paraphernalia turned us all to instant merriment before we finished these sessions.

She arrived to join her bicycle and cabin-trunk with a mountain of further valises, hat boxes, despatch cases and hold-alls, umbrellas, rugs and parcels of en route shopping that took Mr Munday, our asthmatic old taxi driver friend, a considerable time to extract from his evil-smelling old Renault.

After the heart attack that signalled the close of the bicycle season, Gan-Gan was advised to take a glass of port and a Bath Oliver at elevenses as a tonic. Being like all Farquhars strictly teetotal, it had to be Wincarnis and on one occasion my mother ran out of it only to find the Benson grocer had done likewise. Nothing loth she filched a bottle of my father's precious vintage Taylor's which went down a treat for the rest of that visit, ending in Gan-Gan's saying before she left: "That Wincarnis of yours is far better than the stuff I get from Strachans, Madge, could you arrange to have some sent north for me?" Father was livid, Gan-Gan blissfully unaware and clearly much better for the deception.

Roger and I, like all nursery children, were paraded after tea in a painful, polished and tricked-out state for the benefit of all visitors, being either enjoined to keep absolute silence if bridge were in progress or tee-ed up on the pouffe to sing a Lewis Caroll song unaccompanied – agony in any case, though on the whole I preferred whispered asides to piping "*I Have a Little Shadow*" or "*The Spotted Cow all Red and White*". On one such occasion I was transfixed by the mysterious noises made by my father's brother officer, General Chenevix-Trench's new tin leg (he'd lost one in the war) until Clare Hynes, an old Irish friend who was staying with us, in desperation cried "For goodness sake Michael, go and play with your father's throat and leave General Trench's leg alone."

Those were untroubled times, flowing smoothly on an even keel and with a steady tempo of endless people to stay, Christmas parties in the neighbourhood and regular trips to Oxford for lunch at the Randolph Grill before seeing Douglas Fairbanks Senior, the Gish sisters, Rudolph Valentino, and many other silent movie stars at the Electra cinema, or to

Reading when it was the less distinguished Cadena Cafe or Heelas Palm Court Restaurant before flicks at the Vaudeville.

The Christmas holidays were always enlivened by a thrilling visit to Aunt Carry in Cadogan Place for the pantomime and later the current musical comedy or thriller. The former, except only for Peter Pan, invariably had George Robey as the Dame and it was years before we awoke to his plethora of double entendres that so diverted the adults.

My father was a dab-hand at fixing excellent children's parties with clever and varied treasure hunts and always a brilliantly-conceived charade or two to finish with. Added to this he was quite a good conjuror and, best of all, a nine-day wonder when he diverted us by blowing pipe-smoke through his neck whence it came billowing out of his shirt collar. Years later we heard Clare, I think it was, who had been similarly entertained, whispering to her friend, "Come and see Grandpa's hole"! – Plus ça change . . .!

Golf soon came into our lives; I had my first set of mini-clubs when I was seven and in due course my brother and I became junior members of Huntercombe Golf Club, which was later to be immortalised by Dennis Thatcher. The tennis court at the Old Mill House was never much good, but Granny's at Greenhayes next door was alright for our early attempts.

The only occasion that I remember of events outside our cosy orbit interrupting the even tenor of our way was when in 1926 the general strike caused Desmond and me to be returned to Ashdown House in lordly state, driven by Aunt Carry's faithful chauffeur Shepherd in her Rolls. It was Shepherd whose professional guidance was closely followed when some years later we at last became a one-car family, an enormously exciting and never-to-be-forgotten day. It was a maroon 4-door stately Wolseley 15 saloon with the recently patented Triplex safety glass that blistered and steadily acquired a sickly yellow opacity. It also had one of the very stiffest crash gearboxes ever designed, making double declutching gear shifts an attenuated and severe test of strength and skill. We all loved that first precious car and when years later she was sold, my mother wept for weeks and refused to pass the garage where she stood awaiting a new owner. The whole affair resembled something out of *Black Beauty*.

In the early years after the Great War, we usually went with Granny Goodbody in a large family party to the Devon or Cornwall seaside; but later, when I went to prep-school, we started a long series of Scottish summer holidays with Granny St John in Aboyne. These were of such consequence and the many characters involved so diverse and entertaining, that they must form a whole section of my ramblings on their own.

For the present, I must tell you that childhood at Benson was becoming boyhood, the big emancipation coming first with Roger's translation in 1924 to Wellington College in preparation for the army and then my entry in 1929 to the RNC Dartmouth as a naval cadet. We had long been brainwashed into an uncomplicated and total acceptance of these then still highly-regarded martial careers, which were all my parents could with difficulty afford to provide for us.

Greater changes were to follow, for in the depth of the early Depression, Lord Wittenham died and his widow was compelled to sell the Howberry Park Estate. For us this meant a sad farewell to the Old Mill House and I wept bitterly as I took my last, fast-dwindling look at the only home I had known and loved all my 16 years, through the minute rear window of old Mr Munday's rattle-trap en route for the train at Wallingford and my return to Dartmouth.

My Father after his Trachy tube had been removed with me and Roger. 1921.

CHAPTER IV
Adolescence at Henley

The kindness and generosity of the Wittenham's did not die with His Lordship. Fifteen years or more after they first adopted my parents' cause, Lady Wittenham not only continued her late husband's covenant in their favour to help with Roger's and my schooling, but also presented them with a much larger, well-built house and extensive garden high on Harpsden Hill, two miles south of Henley-on-Thames, plus furniture from Howberry Park to fill the extra spaces. Southwood was its name.

After the glories of Queen Anne it was no beauty from the outside, but all the rooms were well-proportioned, spacious, light and airy and it had been built soon after the First World War by an architect who had used only the best materials. Now we had electricity, albeit of our own phut-phut making for the first few years before the mains came our way, as well as central heating.

Instead of the formal gardens of the Old Mill House, we had a wide, irregular and roughly level spread of over four acres that ran back on the north side into mature beech woods soon bursting with drifts of daffodils among the indigenous bluebells. My mother rapidly established shrub and herbaceous borders, roses and ornamental trees and the usual generous vegetable garden. This latter was overlooked by the gardener's cottage-cum-garage-cum-electric-light generating plant and there, eventually, lived Wise, a much younger and more experienced gardener than dear old Mr Harris. He formed a powerful partnership with my mother, being tactful enough not to argue with her but just do as he thought fit behind her back on the rare occasions when their opinions differed. Wise stayed with us till the outbreak of the Second World War when he was called up as an 'Ox and Bucks' LI Terrier. During his time with us he married our housemaid, Gladys, who duly moved across to his cottage from the big house but produced no progeny and continued working for us. I recollect her reporting in tears that he had 'gone to serve overseas' on joining up; this it transpired was to training camp on the Isle of Wight.

With the move to Henley suddenly all was change. Gone were the sleepy, unconcerned quiet and uncomplicated passing of days by the millstream; soon gone also was our first car, the distinguished old Wolseley to give way to a Standard of more recent vintage. And there were many new friends, though we still kept up with some of the old ones beyond Wallingford.

Roger duly became a GC at Sandhurst on his way to join his father's regiment and soon after my seventeenth birthday I would leave the RNC to go to sea in HMS *Dorsetshire*, flag-ship of the Second Cruiser Squadron in the Home Fleet. As is the the happy way with nature, girls ceased to be a dirty word around this time and instead became a welcome distraction, though strictly forbidden fruit in those pre-pill days.

I will touch on some of the more memorable occasions of my pre-war naval service in the next chapter. Enough now to say that *Dorsetshire*, still with Midshipman St John aboard, soon went as flag-ship to the South African Station (later re-termed South Atlantic) from which we returned in 1934.

It happened shortly after this home-coming that my parents were due to motor over to Blackwater to spend the day with their old friends the Godfrey Fells and asked if they might bring me along. "Yes," they said "by all means, and tell him to come ready for tennis as B (their younger daughter Barbara) will take him with her to neighbours of ours who are sure not to mind."

They did not mind and students of astrology might, if they chose to look it up, have found my stars in a very significant conjunction for it was to Arthur and Patience Guinness at Hawley Place that B took me and

Southwood. My first car, the Austin "Square Four". 1935.

where I became instantly and for ever after a welcomed visitor. After tennis that day I was told to mix the drinks – cocktails still very much in fashion – and quite a cheery session ensued (I remember using some Focking in my mixture which did not pass vulgar notice). Into this scene paraded three delightful, demure and beautiful children, a girl and two boys, who having said "How do you do," nicely, escaped with speed. All unknowingly I had met Pam my future wife.

She was not yet nine years old at the time, so naturally it was ten years before our romance flowered. In the meantime I had met at a Hawley party a bevy of stunning ballerinas from Vic/Wells and de Basil's Ballet Russe de Monte Carlo, all staying with a somewhat notoriously rich and loose-living ex-Life Guards officer who had brought them over for drinks. One, in particular, named Brigitte Hartwig – stage name Vera Zorina – I think quite fancied me. Anyway I fell madly in love with her and became an ardent balletomane, spending many weekends at this chap's place at Knaphill running around with her, Tamara Toumanova and Irena Baronova of de Basil's Ballet as well as Margot Fonteyne, Pamela May and Gwyneth Matthews of Vic/Wells. It was a short-lived idyll for Brigitte achieved fame in the West End production of the ballet-burlesque show *On your Toes* and went to Hollywood for Sam Goldwyn. Anyhow, her turgid Norwegian mother had discovered I was not the dead rich English milord she had supposed! Brigitte later became the fifth Mme Georges Ballenchine, while he was choreographing for her in the Ziegfeld Follies at that time.

Back home at Southwood, I found that Granny Goodbody, who had earlier sold Greenhayes and moved first to Wallingford (next door, it turned out, to Agatha Christie) and thence to Oxford, had now come to live alongside us again, down the hill near the Shiplake railway station. Whenever we were apt to sow the odd wild oat, or otherwise find Southwood unavailable, she provided a welcome, never-failing sanctuary from parental wrath or for a nestless fledgling. No questions were ever asked, a sympathetic ear lent and material and spiritual succour generously forthcoming. How lucky we were with such a devoted, self-effacing and intelligent granny! I am glad to say we appreciated our good fortune in full measure and adored her.

As I have mentioned, extended summer holidays were always spent with our St John granny (Gan-Gan) on Deeside in Scotland. So we escaped the invasions and high prices of Henley Regatta week; indeed on two occasions we let Southwood to one of the competing eights and their hangers-on. For the rest of the year there seemed always plenty going on. Almost every morning when we were at home we played golf at Huntercombe or occasionally on the local 18-hole course at the foot of Harpsden Hill on the way into Henley.

As you may know, Huntercombe had been bought by William Morris, of motor-car fame, after he was black-balled at Frilford Heath by the Oxford University GC. He built the magnificent clubhouse with an annexe for himself and Lady Morris to live in, as well as two indoor tennis courts with squash and badminton courts attached. Having done that, he limited membership to those resident within 20 miles (Oxford was just over 20 miles away) and ordained that guests could only play with club members and for some time members of Oxford University were precluded as guests. We often met him out on the course, very sunburned under a French beret or chatting in the bar with his bear-leader Kennerley-Rumford, the club secretary and matinee idol, baritone husband of Dame Clara Butt.

We made our grass tennis court fairly acceptable and had many good parties thereon. Strangely we seldom went on the river at Henley, being so taken up with other pursuits due to the wider scope made possible by our enhanced mobility; first Roger, and then three or four years later myself as a Sub-Lieutenant, acquired cars of our own. Mine was a very fine 1929 Austin 'Square Four' tourer, with very solid, midnight-blue coach work and real leather seats. I had just opened my first bank account with an allowance from my father of £20. The Westminster Bank chief clerk in Henley was a Mr Sivyer who, in accepting my £20, carefully instructed me in the mysteries of a current account, debited the newly-opened account with 10/- for a cheque book and sold me this car which was his for the previously agreed price of £35, accepting my first-ever cheque. Thus I started my banking life overdrawn by £15.10/- and no questions asked. As Mr Sivyer soon became branch manager, I was home and dry for life and only moved my

Southwood. My Mother and Aunt Carrie Rickman

account from the Henley Branch when we finally came to live near Midhurst in 1954, 20 years later. During the war, when my submarine movements were of course top secret, my mother would ask him if I'd been writing any cheques recently. Despite her having no right to do so he usually obliged with the latest date to hand and sometimes a hint of the payee's locality.

I covered a great mileage in that car, mostly between Plymouth, Portsmouth, the RNC Greenwich and several times to Scotland until, on being posted in 1937 to the China Station, I sold her for more than I gave. The new owner was a Shiplake farmer, who removed the handsome coachwork and converted her into a low-loader for collecting the apples in his orchards.

This car was extremely popular with the three Guinness children whenever I was staying at Hawley during the school holidays for they successfully bullied me into allowing them to drive it around the private roads of the Minley Manor estate perched on my knee – it was hilarious fun but not very safe.

These three used to put sixpenny bets on the horses with their friend the local blacksmith and in 1940 Pam won £5 on Bogscar in the National with which they secretly bought an Austin Seven from the groom's brother. They then had to hock Pam's bike for £1 to buy a new battery. They hid the car in a rhododendron bush. Pam procured jerry cans of petrol from the French Canadian troops, thus running a severe risk of being raped and when I was proudly let into the secret I was horrified to find James, aged 15, siphoning petrol by sucking a rubber tube. Having just seen one of my brother officers nearly kill himself by swallowing the stuff and certainly not trusting the 'Vin Doos' I betrayed the children. Sadly I thus lost for many years the trust of my then 12-year old future brother-in-law, Ivan.

On one glorious summer evening, I drove myself in white tie and tails to Oxford for the Brasenose Commemoration Ball and duly followed tradition by being photographed at the party in next morning's 6 am sunshine and a pretty mellow mood. On leaving and realising that there I was on a peerless summer morning in the famous Oxford High quite alone, I pulled up behind a centre island short of Magdalene Bridge and, standing on my driver's seat in the open car, turned back to drink in the renowned beauty of the scene. Alas, the mellow mood was not conducive to stability on a sprung car seat and before I could save myself, I overbalanced and dived head first between the rear seat and the back of the one I had been standing on. I don't suppose that any of my readers have found themselves in this precise position, so I have no hesitation in informing them that the effect is similar to the most devastating wrestling hold imaginable – almost a sort of reverse Boston crab. Anyway, the young policeman, not that much older than myself, who found me thus bouleversé, in full evening dress, giggling weakly and firmly jammed, arse-up, proved very understanding and helped me, with a caution, on my way.

And here Granny Goodbody once more comes to the rescue for I was staying with her in Shiplake, my parents being away and Southwood shut up for the servants' holidays. She produced strong coffee and a warm bed on the instant and had me up and firing again in time to motor to Wimbledon where I had been lent centre court debentures for me and my current girlfriend whom I was to meet for lunch.

In case my readers be tempted to suppose I am sweeping all my lesser moments under the carpet, I will confess to one other event in which the Austin took part and which I trust may stand as an effective warning to my younger readers. I drove up from Henley for the celebration dinner my group of Sub-Lieutenants had arranged in a private room at the Criterion Restaurant in Piccadilly Circus to mark our passing out from the RNC Greenwich. Together with a mate with whom I'd agreed a mutual protection pledge against the dangers of the night, I'd booked into the Hammam Turkish Baths (in those days 12/6d for the night all found) and thither repaired by taxi to drop off my overnight bag after safely parking the car at Moon's Garage near Olympia. The Hammam Baths in Jermyn Street belonged to Penhaligons, my hairdressers then around the corner in Bury Street, and unlike the nearby Savoy Baths were highly respectable and a great refuge for penniless young men. Alas, together with the Old Cavendish Hotel and most of Quaglinos they were demolished by a direct hit during the Blitz and never rose again.

As you might expect, we had a riotous evening, much wine flowing at dinner, and thereafter in groups we scattered to various haunts from 'The 400' to 'The Bag of Nails' according to taste. My friend and I, plus a third Sub-Lieutenant, ended up listening enraptured to splendid jazz on the piano of Garnons Wilson at the Coconut Grove, warmed by the contents of three-quarters of a bottle of brandy that our Number Three, a member of 'The Grove', happily remembered was in his locker. This Number Three, a notorious satyr, was soon off with a pretty floozie, leaving the pair of us to kill his bottle in what seemed a short time. All was bliss until we hit the chill wind of a dark, wet and stormy November night at about 3 am. From this moment on I have only my friend's word for what ensued, as the next I knew I was lying, freezing to death and covered in London mud under a rug in the back of my car, which was standing in the dead centre of the road on the town side of Henley bridge. A grey, watery dawn was breaking and the friend was hurling gravel at the windows of the Crown Inn without effect. Fighting back nausea and a splitting headache, I urged him to try the Catherine Wheel a little further up the street. Here mercy in the form of a sympathetic night-porter came to our rescue. He got us to bed in a double room, having helped us to undress and taken all our clothes to clean as best he might.

It appears that on emerging into Upper Regent Street, I had instantly measured my length into the teeming gutter and the friend, himself undergoing severe gyro-failure but still with his wits somewhere at hand, salvaged me and managed in a series of wild spiralling dashes to get us both across Piccadilly and into Jermyn Street. He related that here, and in sight of the Hammam Bath's night-watchman, I declared I wanted to pee. He duly propped me against a lamp-post, helped to point the equipment in question towards a road drain and waited. Nothing – I was giggling so wildly that I'd acquired what I believe is termed 'hysterical retention'. He tried to whistle, but was laughing so much himself he failed. Nothing loth, he invited two tarts who had been enjoying the show to whistle for us, which they did producing instant results to warm applause and much hilarity. Alas, all this tamasha had been witnessed by the night-watchman who firmly collected our bags and loaded us into the Hammam's tame taxi for drunks. The friend, having purloined my wallet to reward the lady whistlers with one of my precious remaining 10/- notes, also found my Moon's Garage car ticket. Miraculously he drove on the centre white line all the way to Henley. We arranged for a 9 o'clock call at the hotel and, climbing back into our roughly sponged-off DJs and with hotel face-towels concealing the absence of our ruined, boiled shirts beneath, we left tips and thanks and set off with me at the wheel this time to put my friend on a train back to London. He was due to report to his rich uncle and guardian in Prince's Gate (his father was killed in the war and he had been a King's Cadet at Dartmouth) in order to discuss his allowance. Luckily, the uncle proved liberal and understanding and I crept to Granny's as I dared not appear in that doleful condition at Southwood! God Bless Granny, and I have ever since kept my solemn promise to her never again to pass out from alcohol. We all may do it once, but thereafter one should know the warning signs and it should never happen twice.

We had many visitors during these, for me, emergent years: both relations, happily including Uncle Andy on his annual progress in the south, and a wide variety of my parents' friends as well as Roger's and mine. Uncle Andy made his headquarters at the 'In and Out' from where he generously entertained his younger relations to London shows and sallied forth visiting relations, spending at least one week with us. His wardrobe remained unaltered from his Aboyne habits: a Lovat green plus-two suit with black hobnailed brogues in the country and an ill-fitting chocolate brown serge suit and homburg hat for London. After the war, having given up his club, he put up at the Basil Street Hotel where he rapidly became a feature as 'the Commander' on his regular pilgrimages. It was from here that he made the understandable, but disastrous mistake of taking Roger's daughters and 'The Merry Widow' with whom he had forever been hopelessly in love, to see *The Killing of Sister George* thinking it was a thriller – my nieces were entranced by both the play which they could not understand and the widow's horror, but chiefly by the latter. I shall describe this predatory lady later.

The last big Southwood house-party I took part in was an hilarious weekend riot to celebrate my twenty-first birthday, when the house was filled with my particular brother-officers and sundry girlfriends. Jimmy Dundas was there and the piano, plus Roger's drums, was never silent from dawn to the ensuing small hours. Soon after that, having completed my submarine training course at Blockhouse, I was posted to HMS/M Pandora in the Fourth Flotilla on the China Station.

The next time I saw Southwood was in November 1939 on my wartime return from the Far East to a blacked-out England. It was to be the last occasion, for my father a little later contracted serious phlebitis while fishing in Scotland and never returned to Henley. He was invalided from his House of Commons job and having chosen to end his days in his childhood environs on Deeside, Southwood and Granny's Shiplake house were sold.

At 24 years old I was now a fully-fledged Submariner and before the year was out had qualified as a Commanding Officer. Those of us who were lucky enough to come through unscathed usually dislike dwelling on the war years – tragic, profitless, bloody and frequently extremely frightening, they consumed the best part of my twenties, spanned the loss of many of my closest friends and so far as I am concerned are best forgotten.

Hermione Slessor, Arthur Guinness's cousin, told my fortune one day early in 1940 at Hawley Place. She said I would survive the war, get happily married and have three children. Who dares say No to ESP? Here we all are – me, Pam, Andrew, Clare and Hermione, who was named after the sybil.

R.N.C. Dartmouth Sunday Divisions, 1933

CHAPTER V
A decade of naval occasions
1929 to 1939

While I was there from 1929 to 1932, the RNC Dartmouth, and the entry thereto, were little changed from the rigorous pattern ordained by that fearsome, so-called 'Father of the Modern Navy', Jackie Fisher. He himself relates in his autobiography that when he joined at the age of 12, he was sent off alone by train in charge of the guard to Portsmouth, where he was delivered to the hall porter of the Keppel's Head on the Hard (known to all NO's as 'The Nut'). The following morning he was collected by a naval messenger, taken to the Flag Officer Portsmouth's residence in the dockyard and ushered into the august presence of the incumbent and the Senior (doubtless Irish and bucolic) Medical Officer. The former ordered him to recite the Lord's Prayer and after he had successfully done so, the SMO told him to strip off to the buff and "jump over that chair". The naked young Jackie duly leapt, got dressed and was congratulated on winning his entry into the Royal Navy.

What a contrast to the formidable process with which he inaugurated us. First, a very full medical in front of opthalmic, dental and ENT consultants amongst a plethora of disagreeable, thoroughly bored MOs – there was, thank heaven, no trick-cycling in those days. Every crevice was explored, and we were made to do rigorous exercises in the nude (in front of a blazing fire in my case, which scorched my bum as I obeyed the order to 'double knees bend') plus endless questions about past illnesses.

This obstacle overcome, you later faced the dreaded Interview in the old buildings of the Admiralty, escorted thither by your prep-school headmaster. We were first dumped in a poky, windowless cubby-hole with pen and paper and told to write an essay in ten minutes, in my case on "What do you consider to be the attributes of a perfect uncle?" I feel sure my effort was as futile as the subject and naturally your wits were wildly scattered in the face of the ordeal to come. It felt as if you were in the Condemned Cell, awaiting the chaplain's entrance. Then came the final appalling shock – to be pushed haltingly by a messenger into a vast room across the end of which sat a bevy of, to us, Methuselahs, staring fixedly at their next victim across a long green-baize covered table. To one side, on an easel, hung a large map of the world with all the extant countries marked and many blobs for towns; the rivers and mountains also shown, but not a single name. You sat alone on a chair facing the Methuselahs, all indistinguishable in dark London suits. It transpired that they included in their number a public-school headmaster, a top civil servant and a bevy of admirals.

Already in a state of shock, the next blow swiftly fell when the leading Methuselah opened proceedings by producing your putrid essay with the ink still wet, concerning which he started the bowling by asking you to enlarge on your facetious points. That done and by now no better than a jelly, you were ordered to your feet, given a pointer and told to stand by the easel and indicate on the board the location of the various geographical features they named in rapid succession. I sometimes wonder what the European Court of Human Rights would have made of this slow assassination of a lone 12-year old.

However, having thus demolished you the Methuselahs became kindly and avuncular and at a less hectic speed, asked all sorts of quasi-interested questions, some obvious – "Why have you chosen the Navy?" – some silly – "What was the number of the taxi you came in?" – and some, I suppose, loaded. Anyhow, by the time they let you go they were all smiling and wished you well as you crept away, to be swiftly cross-examined by your prep-school headmaster about your answers. I have never discovered how many failed the interview, but I understand they weeded out a noticeable percentage.

A TALE OF TWO RIVERS

Those lucky ones who passed these two rigorous tests (about half the original number of candidates, I believe) now sat the Navy Entrance Exam, different and tougher than Common Entrance, as witnessed by the fact that extra tuition, particularly in maths, was necessary. You advisedly went to a prep-school that claimed to specialise in preparing naval candidates. You also sat CE as a safety-belt. I believe that in my term there were, at the start, over 600 candidates for only 43 vacancies, such in those days was the esteem and popularity of Britain's senior service.

The exam took place in the University of London's Bloomsbury Headquarters and the ubiquitous naval tailors, Gieves, set up an elaborate reception area in the nearby Russell Hotel, where they measured and fitted all the candidates with their uniforms regardless of whether they would pass or fail. They sold the entire very costly list laid down by Their Lordships; the lot, including sports gear, luggage and a handsome navy-blue rug embroidered with your initials in large red letters, for everything had to be uniform. The cost was over £150, the equivalent now I guess of £4,000 plus. It was a crafty piece of enterprise which captured as future customers at least 90% of the officer strength of the entire service and beggared your parents in the process. In return, they sent you a telegram of congratulations on passing that arrived 24 hours in advance of Their Lordships' notification.

Once in, you faced eleven terms of the most rigorous discipline and intense cramming in an establishment from which all women were debarred, except for the dragon-like Naval Nursing Sisters in the hospital.

The classics, having been included in the exam, were dropped; in their place came naval engineering, seamanship, navigation and naval as well as general history. The procedure was: cold salt-water plunges at dawn; divisions with rifles on the parade ground after breakfast; marched in a squad at the double from study to study; forbidden to talk to any cadet other than your own term, i.e. those who joined with you and thereafter shared the same dormitories and gun-rooms. It was in the latter that your sparse leisure was spent and where you did early school (6.30 am in summer, 7.00 am in winter) and an hour's evening prep after supper. Even turning-in or getting-up was done by numbers, including the order "Say your prayers" which entailed your standing silently to attention by your sea-chest when finished until the term's religious maniac had reeled off several novenas or whatever; a great nuisance which did nothing for our piety as we only had ten minutes to plunge, wash and get into uniform. At night every item of clothing had to be folded to exact measurements and stowed in a set manner in your sea-chest. Finally the Officer of the Day, preceded by a bugler did Rounds and as he and his entourage swept through your dormitory, believe it or not, we had to lie to attention, in our beds. To compensate somewhat for this harsh regime, the college buildings and equipment were superb and we had a vast staff of eminent tutors plus a full complement of carefully selected naval officers to push us along. We had excellent playing fields and sports facilities, a huge gymnasium complex staffed by PTIs; equally well-staffed engineering workshops and, of course, hundreds of boats on the River Dart, all supervised by hand-picked retired Petty Officer instructors – and what memorable and outstanding characters they were.

Their Lordships and indeed your parents spared no expense in those days when the Royal Navy was still paramount in our defences and Britain continued to rule the waves.

I have already mentioned that I went to sea in 1932, a few months past my seventeenth birthday, joining the county class cruiser *Dorsetshire* in the Home Fleet. It was just after the notorious Invergordon Mutiny which rocked the civilised world and helped to take Great Britain off the Gold Standard. It was a disgraceful affair and even then, in the depths of the slump, most people's sympathy was with the sailors. Their Lordships, without any prior notice issued an Admiralty Fleet Order ordaining without explanation that the sailors' pay was there and then to be reduced by 1/- a day – a very considerable chunk of what had never been a generous treasury hand-out in the first place.

Fortunately, the officers of the Home Fleet acted with speed, tact and considerable skill and by the time I joined, the trouble was already overcome and the very popular Admiral, Jo Kelly, appointed Commander-in-Chief to mend the fences, which he did with great aplomb.

Immediately I had joined, the Second Cruiser Squadron, which comprised *Dorsetshire* flying the flag of CS2, *York* and *Cumberland*, sailed from Devonport at the start of the summer cruise to attend the British Fair in Copenhagen. This was a very prestigious affair with, in addition to the three 10,000 ton cruisers, a company of the Gordon Highlanders with their Regimental Pipes and Band, all led by HRH The Prince of Wales to boost our cause. The beauties of Copenhagen are well-known and arriving as we did on a calm, sunny summer morning was something never to be forgotten. We escorted the Danish King in his royal yacht, dressed overall into that beautiful harbour with its stunning waterfront framing Hans Anderson's Little Mermaid and the magnificent Lange-Ligne alongside which all three ships secured. I can still vividly recall, after 50 years, the clean fresh air, aromatic with the smell of coffee roasting and the flowers blooming behind the wharves in the Lange-Ligne gardens. The myriad bicycles too – all Denmark seemed to be on bikes, including the girls who coasted in summer frocks down the hill in line abreast to see the British matelôts. In harbour, officers and Snotties-of-the-Watch on the quarterdeck, frock-coated and in bum-freezers respectively, always carried telescopes and it passed the time aboard *Dorsetshire* to suddenly whip our telescopes to our eyes and train them on these Gigis as they free-wheeled towards us. This had the delightful effect of causing them, in panic, to grab their skirts to stop them from blowing up in the wind and often as not in consequence, to run into each other and end bottoms up in the road.

In those heady days, visiting NOs were thoroughly spoilt – honorary membership of all the best clubs, endless parties where nubile daughters were anxious to please, outings to all features including Tivoli Gardens, the Royal Copenhagen Potteries, the Tuborg and Carlsberg breweries and the newly-formed Royal Copenhagen Golf Club at nearby Klampenbörg. It was here that I made local history by performing what was quickly dubbed 'The Prince of Wales shot' which threatened to become immortal.

A fellow cadet friend and I had put our names down for the British Officers' team to play a match against the Royal Copenhagen Club and to our surprise had been selected. HRH, a keen golfer, was our captain and declared that we would tee-off in reverse order of Navy List seniority –

that meant Basil Ward and me opening the day in front of a vast crowd of local notables and ambitious beauties hanging round the Prince, plus the players (24 a side) and the world press in force. Basil and I tossed for who should go first, since as visitors we were accorded this (unwanted) honour, and I lost. With quaking knees, dumb with fright, I duly teed-up to hit the first shot of the day, shut my eyes and swiftly took an almighty swipe. The tip of my driver made telling impact, sending the ball at maximum velocity at right-angles to the intended line of flight and into the wooden tee-box. Gaining added kinetic energy from this collision it shot past my right ear with a piercing rush of sibilance, quickly drowned by a concerted gasp of horror from the crowd behind me.

On turning round I discovered HRH in fits of laughter being helped from the ground by two of his attendant floosies whence he had been hurled by a quick-acting detective to get him out of the direct line of my sadly misguided missile. Regicide before my eighteenth birthday – what price fame.

Nor was that the end of my achievement that day. Klampenbörg still awaited the completion of a proper clubhouse and the locker rooms were housed in a dark log cabin where one mucked in as best one could. As my match approached the ninth hole and, having been first away was farthest from home, a devasting thunder-storm put an end to the game and all rushed for shelter in this inadequate building. Last in, and more soaked than anyone else, I groped my way through steaming golfers in semi-darkness to where beneath a murky window I had left what few extra clothes I possessed on a chair. I was annoyed to find that someone had deposited their large and expensive-looking suitcase on top of my things, so I quickly removed it and dumped it with little ceremony and a muttered curse on the floor. Instantly there was a gasp of horror close beside me and I espied a pair of striped trousers which rose to a Marlboro' jacket topped by an ashen countenance. It was the ultimate Jeeves holding beautifully pressed clothes over one arm. Turning in wild confusion, I saw a man struggling out of his wet shirt on the other side of me.

You have rightly guessed. I was between the heir apparent and his valet and had just chucked his suitcase on the floor. On seeing me and what I had done, he again burst out laughing and said something to the effect that "it's you again Snottie, and I bet you've no change of clothes. I remember my days in the Gunroom, when everyone pinched everyone else's gear," and then turning to his man, "Give this young gentleman a pullover, I've got plenty to spare." Accepting this rare gift I mumbled my thanks and groped my way to a less rarified quarter – after all, he was not only the Prince of Wales, but an Admiral of the Fleet and I a mere worm of a cadet.

Word soon spread concerning this event and back on board I was summoned by the Fleet Engineer Officer and commanded to surrender the royal pullover to him so that he, God alone knows why, could return it to its august owner. He was about the most notorious and objectionable snob in the entire navy and having said so, I refrain from naming him. I bet he kept the damned thing. It follows that he was no friend of mine and I later got a measure of revenge as Snottie-of-the-Watch at anchor off Lossiemouth when I allowed him to climb, laden with his golf-clubs, down the 30-foot port side of the ship on a Jacob's ladder into a motor-boat. This, he fancied, had been ordered specially to take him ashore for a round on the local links (he was always demanding special boats to the discomfort of the Midshipmen and their boats' crews). As soon as he gained its stern-sheets, the boat shoved off and went round to the starboard side where it was hoisted inboard on the seaplane crane. It had been sent in for the mail and with the FEO as super-cargo was now unloaded from its cradle on the boat-deck since it had proved too rough for Postie to get the mailbags up the Jacob's ladder. The manner in which I then told him that his boat was alongside the starboard gangway left him in no doubt about my earlier reticence and present pleasure.

We had ten glorious days at Copenhagen before reluctantly sailing to join the fleet for the annual plethora of exercises and hard graft at Scapa-Flow. We were a happy ship, but in those days the life of a very junior gunroom officer was, by and large, hell. We were treated like dirt by everyone, beaten on all possible pretexts, and made to perform the most menial tasks, cleaning brightwork and scrubbing decks. We survived, somehow, unscathed and as doubtless intended, it made us ever after aware of the worst hardships of the lower deck.

As my time progressed things got a bit easier; the navy was even yet emerging from its pre-war narrowness and the rigours of the days of sail. First, we acquired with great good fortune a new Admiral, Percy Noble, renowned as the best-dressed man in the fleet, who occasionally had us to dinner in the cuddy where we played vingt-et-un with him and lost. After visiting Gib, Majorca, Madeira and the Canary Islands the following spring, *Dorsetshire* was paid off into dockyard hands at Devonport and Percy Noble sent for each of us to ask what we would like to do next. We all said we would like to stay in *Dorsetshire* for we knew she was due to be flagship on the South Atlantic Station based at Simonstown. He duly fixed this for us and two years later, in 1935, long after we had returned to UK from the Cape, I was in the crowd outside the west stand at Twickenham before the Army/Navy match, when Sir Percy, immaculate in bowler and a red carnation in his overcoat, came past with the Duke of Gloucester whom, as Fourth Sea Lord, he was helping to escort. Recognising me at a distance after all that time, he broke away and came over to say "Hullo, St John, did you have a good time in South Africa?" What a great gift to remember your most junior of juniors like that. It makes for hero worship. Later again, in 1937, he was Commander-in-Chief China and once more remembered me when I joined the Fourth Submarine Flotilla and had me to lots of very enjoyable occasions.

I was able to tell him at Twickenham that South Africa had been wonderful. We were swiftly up-'omers in the renowned Capetown suburbs (sailors' parlance to describe being welcome in the local inhabitants' family homes), members of all the clubs, country and otherwise, everywhere we went. We visited all the chief ports from Freetown, Sierra Leone on the West to Beira in Portuguese East on the other; representing an incredible range of climate, ambience and experience. Amongst the latter were rugger at Lagos in 90°F and 100% humidity; touring the prison in Accra, including the occupied condemned cells; and an awful, audible dummy-run on the gallows using a sack, which made me an instant and confirmed capital punishment abolitionist. We sailed up the Congo to Banana past floating islands so big they had forest trees growing on them; to Saldanah Bay, a desolate whaling station waste, Capetown itself, of course, then round Cape Agulhas to East London, Knysna, Port Elizabeth and above all, Durban at the height of the season in July week with the July handicap, South Africa's Derby, and champagne flowing at the Durban Club Ball.

At Lorenzo-Marques (now renamed Maputo) our Admiral, Teddy Evans of the Broke, later Lord Mountevans, was lent the Portuguese Governor's special train in which he took some of us up into the then newly-developed Kruger National Park, north of Swaziland. We lived aboard the train in a siding at Skukusa, which was at that time a collection of mud rondavels, and were taken by the wardens all over the reserve two days before it was open to the public. It was an unforgettable experience; we saw masses of game, including of course the big five, and fell asleep each night to the roaring of the lions coming past to drink at the Lower Swabi River.

Christmas was always spent in Simonstown and during the season the Navy was entertained in force by the fruit farmers of the beautiful Berg River valley near Stellenbosch, who played us at cricket, tennis and rugger. They produced a massive alfresco feast and sent us back loaded to the gunwhales with peaches. One year, I and another Midshipman spent Christmas camping beside the Berg River with our divisional officers and a marine servant, and it was here that I became infatuated with the teenage daughter of the ex-Royal Marine farmer on whose land we were encamped. She and others with whom I frolicked in those far-off, halcyon days I met again not long ago on holiday at the Cape – all like myself with grandchildren, but all essentially unchanged and as charming as ever.

We were lucky to be in South Africa in those days of its dominion status before the onset of the Bröderbond and the infamous system of apartheid that now threatens to explode and blow that beautiful vast country to smithereens. Lucky too to meet the greatest of soldier/statesmen, Jan Smuts, who one day took us midshipmen on foot full tilt to the top of Table Mountain and left us gasping.

I ended my gunroom days back in the home fleet in HMS *Leander* –

once again in the Second Cruiser Squadron in time to take part in George V's Jubilee Review at Spithead where the entire Home, Mediterranean and Reserve Fleets were anchored. It was to be the last time that so many warships would gather in one place and it was truly memorable. It was also renowned as the occasion of Alexander Woodruff's broadcast from HMS *Nelson* when, in describing the fireworks after a fine mess guest-night, he bibulously declared "The fleet'sh lit up, I'm lit up – we're all lit up!", or something to that effect.

Here I successfully passed my seamanship exam, the final hurdle that lay between you and your first stripe as an Acting Sub-Lieutenant. Two and a half years at sea surely broadened the late teenage mind, liberalised one's outlook and showed you, in my case, many foreign parts and their so diverse inhabitants – all good training in becoming a citizen of the world, but quite certainly not conducive to academic progress.

By that time I, like most other NOs, found I had forgotten much of what had been hurled at me at Dartmouth and so we now faced the much needed cross between a brush-up and a smattering of further education at the RNC Greenwich. King George V died while we were there and we had swiftly to get our new cocked hats, epaulettes and dress sword-belts from Gieves where, on the day of his funeral, we attended a service in the beautiful Inigo Jones chapel that stands opposite the Painted Hall. It was a fine sight, full of several hundreds of frock-coated officers bedecked in navy blue and gold braid. I had earlier been to the lying-in-state in Westminster Hall with my father, who took me and some friends in through the private members' entrance, while the four Royal sons were standing guard at the catafalque. It was immensely impressive and is stamped indelibly on my memory – the vivid splash of colour of the floodlit catafalque and the full-dress uniforms in the midst of that vast, empty and otherwise darkened place with not a sound to be heard or a movement to distract the mind from the solemn stillness.

Despite being so close to the flesh-pots of the West End – we all had cars of some sort in which to get there – we did manage to absorb some more naval history, applied maths and French before moving to Pompey. There, the next 18 months were divided between courses in gunnery, navigation, signals and torpedo/anti-submarine warfare at their respective schools. Once through you were confirmed in the rank of Sub-Lieutenant, your seniority depending on the results of the five exams you had taken, starting with seamanship. It was at this point that Their Lordships finding themselves short of three volunteers for the submarine service from my year, split us into three seniority groups and picked a name out of each. I was the one to emerge from the top third and moved heaven and earth to get out of it as I'd set my heart on becoming a navigator. But to no avail.

I duly joined HMS *Dolphin* at Fort Blockhouse and at once realised my luck. The submarine service was and remains a superb private navy in which all who joined swiftly felt proud and happy to serve, and in which I was destined to enjoy the next ten or more years, making a host of lifelong friends and, alas, losing so many in the war.

On qualifying, I was as I have mentioned appointed to *Pandora* in the Fourth Flotilla in China and with four other Fourth Hands set sail in great luxury aboard the P&O mail-ship *Carthage*, visiting Gib for Edward VIII's coronation parade, Marseille where we experienced bouillabaise and blue cinemas; Malta, with lots of naval friends; the Suez Canal; Aden (awful); Bombay (smelly); Colombo (beautiful); Penang (likewise); Singapore, with Happy Valley and Raffles; Hong Kong, with more naval friends; and finally, after six weeks of sybaritic comfort to Shanghai. Here we stayed as guests in the Shanghai Club with its famous Long Bar, before transferring to a Butterfield and Swire China boat that took us north via Tsing Tao to Wei-hai-Wei, where at last we joined the China fleet and our respective boats.

Lots of adventures came our way on that voyage, both on board and ashore, of which perhaps the coronation parade at Gib merits a mention in greater detail. The Flag Officer Gib, who was taking the parade, elected to do so mounted and his naval staff perforce did likewise perched dangerously on polo ponies that also regularly took part in the Calpe Hunt Races. The signal for the climactic 'Advance in Review Order' was given by a Yeoman of Signals to one side of the saluting base smartly bringing to the ground the flag A that he had been holding aloft on a staff. The signal to start the Calpe Races was likewise made by lowering a flag. So, on hearing the sharp flutter of the Yeoman's signal, the entire

Reviewing Officer's mounted entourage took off, cocked hats and all, at full gallop straight towards the advancing ranks of sailors whose centre they scattered to the winds before completing a few circuits of the parade ground. We had landed as spectators of this event and could not have wished for better free entertainment. We had a fine run ashore with many naval friends that day, celebrating the occasion at the Rock and Bristol bars, ending up jumping from my cousin Bobby Farquhar's boat whose destroyer was in harbour onto a Jacob's ladder after *Carthage* was under way. The Master was displeased by this embarkation but the onlooking passengers crowded the guard-rails to enjoy the show.

For the next two years I was able to enjoy all the delights of an unspoilt China Station that stretched from Penang in the south west to Peking in the north and included Borneo, the Philippines and Celebes as well as what is now Indonesia.

As a Lieutenant on about £450 per annum naval pay, I was a member of 25 clubs, owned a Ford V8 roadster in Hong Kong and when there regularly took a girlfriend to dinner and dance (to A1 Philippino Jazz) at one of the big hotel restaurants once or twice a week. There were endless bathing picnics, shooting of pigeon in the New Territories and snipe at Wei-hai-Wei, golf and tennis everywhere we went and I played rugger and hockey for the Navy at Happy Valley in the Hong Kong triangular tournament – Navy, Army and Hong Kong – which we consistently won, since the China Fleet was very large in those days. I experienced two typhoons, one ashore in Hong Kong when my submarine was refitting; the worst then on record with the anemometer off the scale at 120 knots and wrecks everywhere. The other one came on passage east of the Yangtze estuary, a very unpleasant experience since we could not risk diving in such conditions and perforce rode it out, going slap through the huge, steep waves like a bodkin through a bolster. We registered over 30 feet on the control room depth-gauges and everyone on the bridge had to be securely harnessed and able to hold their breath for what seemed ages.

There were few places in the Far East and South East Asia that I did not visit during those two years: Penang, the Dindings and Port Swettenham (from whence we had a run up to Kuala Lumpur with the local planters – real Somerset Maugham stuff); Singapore, of course, to the new naval base in the Johore Strait; Surabaya, the Dutch East Indies capital of Java; and a heavenly few days in unspoilt and utterly idyllic Bali. In Bali, *Medway* our depot-ship, anchored in a bay on the east coast of this beautiful island, which is as yet mercifully untouched by western soi-disant civilisation, with six submarines alongside. We were immediately surrounded by hundreds of beautiful Balinese in canoes, the girls in their smartest sarongs and bubby jackets, all smiling and waving to the sailors lining the guard rails or illegally poking their heads out of the mess-deck scuttles. Much sign-language activity led to the throwing of anything from gym shoes to cap ribbons and cash, down to the canoes as bribes for the girls to go topless, their boyfriends loyally retrieving the bribes while they readily obliged. Of course, on going ashore later Jolly Jack discovered them all walking gracefully about topless anyway. They only put on bubby jackets for Sunday best.

Returning from Bali we called at the tiny port of Jesselton, in North Borneo, where we made another excursion by the funny little local train to Bathurst with more lonely rubber planters and their dusky wives and children. Thence to Manila, as guests of the US navy who, being forbidden liquor on board, could only think of getting blind drunk ashore and consequently into trouble – and us with them if we didn't take care. They threw a dance in their luxurious Navy Club in our honour at which I was told by a bossy British CO to dance with the formidably upholstered US commodore's wife. She was vast, her hair nailed up with many metal fixtures in an elaborate hair-do and she was heavily gowned like Mrs Hackenbush in the Marx Brothers' *Night at the Opera*. No sooner had I got her moving than I realised she was already legless and I was rapidly becoming so from inhaling the wafts of Bourbon that enveloped me. I did my best and I was a fit second row forward in those days, but she was too much for me. In front of the entire US Subron Five and UK Fourth Submarine Flotilla and almost at her husband's feet, she slowly and relentlessly heeled over, taking me with her in her iron grip. We ended in one almighty crash with hair-pins flying. No-one came to my aid, but I finally got her vertical to resemble a war-torn Valkyrie. Luckily she and everyone else laughed. Apparently, she was often like that.

A TALE OF TWO RIVERS

North of Hong Kong (our base, of course) I visited Amoy and Swatow as well as Tsing-Tao, Wei-hai (our other base) and finally Ching-wang-Tao, the sea-port for Tientsin and Peking, with the Forbidden City, the scene of a great part of the Boxer Rising of 1901.

In 1937/39 there was only one high-rise building on Hong Kong Island, the then brand new Hong Kong and Shanghai Bank; but now this is well nigh invisible in a hideous outbreak of sky-scrapers crammed together in claustrophobic profusion. Across the beautiful harbour only the Peninsular Hotel in Kowloon had more than two or three storeys in those days and the town ended abruptly in unspoilt countryside at the end of Nathan Road. The whole Peak was like a vast wild garden dotted with the best examples of Victorian/Edwardian colonial architecture; and beyond Happy Valley to the east and West Point on the other side the town stopped and it was country all the way to Shek-ho, Stanley and Repulse Bay or to Aberdeen Harbour in the other direction.

A year ago, when I returned on a stop-over en route from Sydney to UK, I almost wept to see the rape that Mammon had committed; it was like the worst nightmare trying to find just one well-remembered feature. Open country and the charming Chinese villages of the New Territories have disappeared and become what must now rank as one of the world's greatest areas of deprivation and ugliness, a high-rise-cum-spaghetti-junction grey, concrete jungle.

But back to pre-war days when there lay in the centre of Hong Kong town Lyndhurst Terrace, the officers-only street of shame, in which were situated the impeccably run maisons tolérées of Rosalie and Ethel. Their fame had long since become legendary throughout the Services, and they deserve a word or two in remembrance from me. They were very socially-minded women and, while always discreet, liked to be seen about at the races or rugger and cricket matches and such.

Rosalie had a spaniel that she let off its lead in the stand at rugger matches in Happy Valley causing endless merriment and red faces as it rushed up with wagging tail to the friends it recognised, including, on one occasion when I was playing in the Triangular Tournament, Admiral Sir Percy Noble himself seated on the touchline in a wicker armchair beside his Lady.

A TALE OF TWO RIVERS

Ethel once had trouble with a nasty naval officer who took passage home to UK without redeeming his chits. You signed chits for everything ashore, including the delights of the Lyndhurst Ladies, and this brute had no less than four outstanding that Ethel's schroff (ie money collector) had brought back from his monthly settlement excursion round the Colony. She went to see the Commodore Hong Kong in the naval dockyard, who gave her several strong drinks, but had to say her only remedy was to write to the culprit c/o The Admiralty – a potentially fruitless pursuit. A few weeks later she ran into Commodore Dicken, a very liberal-minded ex-Naval Attaché in Paris, and hailed him in triumph. She had gone to matins in the cathedral, she told him, and put all the offender's signed chits (they were all of the same universally accepted IOU format) into the offertory box "for the fabric of the cathedral". "I don't mind my girls working for charity," she stoutly declared, "but I'll be fucked if they work for nothing!" Imagine the culprit's surprise on finding his pay debited at source and receiving a warm letter of thanks from the Dean and Chapter. Rosalie and Ethel had large, warm hearts and were full of kindness and good humour. Alas, they both perished at the hands of the Japanese after the fall of Hong Kong.

But on a respectable note, I am pleased to relate that by happy chance my brother Roger, now an Army Captain, was posted as ADC to General Grassett, the GOC China, and arrived at Flagstaff House only a few months after me. We thus shared many happy occasions together until the outbreak of war and indeed, it was there that he met Rosie Vickers, whom he was later to marry. She was staying with her Uncle, Sir Valentine Vandeleur-Grayburn, the Tai-Pan of the Hong Kong and Shanghai Bank, as a companion to his very effervescent and delightfully nubile 17-year old daughter Liz, who was causing much worry to her dad as well as much pleasure to the likes of us.

Munich came and went. The Japanese took over Wei-hai-Wei in 1938 when our lease expired and soon it was 3 September 1939. Having done my stint in *Pandora*, I had just been relieved and was due to return to the UK. Instead I joined *Olympus* which sailed from Johore on an extended patrol that took us from the Lombok Strait, through the

Malacca Strait and the Bay of Bengal to Trincomalee. On return to Singapore I was finally recalled to the UK and sailed home in the troopship *Dilwara* to the blacked-out return to Henley that ended my previous chapter.

I have skimmed over these happy pre-war times and as I re-read what I have written, it is clear to me that I have barely scratched the surface of a deep and diverse store of experience and anecdote, some happy, some hilarious and some sad. Occasions rush to heap themselves in confusion in my memory, but I reckon I have created a fairly accurate pastiche and related enough of the more memorable episodes. So I now turn my efforts to other recollections and not least towards Scotland and the summer holidays that so enhanced my boyhood, dallying en route with Great-Aunt Alice and her daughter Audley's family, the Chapmans.

With my Ford V8 en route to Fan Ling Golf Club. Hong Kong New Territories, 1937.

Entreacte

CHAPTER VI
Aunt Alice and the Chapmans

My St John grandmother's youngest sister, Great-Aunt Alice Thursby-Pelham, and her family were so involved in our lives that they merit a chapter to themselves. I have been puzzled where and how to fit them into these recollections for both in Scotland and the South, from my earliest days till almost the present, they remained very much part of our life.

Having produced two remarkable daughters for him, Aunt Alice obtained a generous separation from her well-to-do and charming husband Jim Thursby-Pelham and proceeded to live an inexcusably selfish life. This she got away with by a combination of the good-looking vivacity and charm that overlaid her steely devotion to her own particular interests and a generous allowance of Scottish guile. But she did have a great feeling for 'Family' and she was always affectionate even when at her most outrageous.

Jim remained a welcome friend of everyone and particularly of my father. They were fellow members of the very exclusive St James's Square Club, Arthur's, renowned for its comfort and good food, the latter served in unusual tradition by maids in mob-caps and aprons. It also boasted one of the best cellars, but all alas has long since disappeared. Jim's collection of antique furniture, paintings and miniatures in his London house in Pelham Crescent was justly famous (his broken-fronted Sheraton bookcase, for instance, was illustrated in the *Encyclopaedia Britannica* of his day) and to the extent that he had set up a special emergency procedure with the main London dealers. They kept at the ready a collection of suitable, comparatively unimportant substitutes that were rushed round to replace his most valuable items whenever Queen Mary, as was often the case, invited herself at short notice for tea. Her Majesty's naughty habit was to admire her host's selected possessions thereby expecting that they would be loyally offered to the royal guest. Such offers were never refused and since the old girl was hot on the subject she acquired a magnificent collection in Marlborough House during a long lifetime of cadging. Jim was a charming dilettante Edwardian, full of good humour and good living. It was always fun meeting Uncle Jim for he was aptly named, my recollections of our encounters being nothing if not sunny.

The two daughters were the beautiful violet-eyed Dolly, who married and divorced a trio of wealthy swains, and the dark, aquiline and handsome Audley who married and stuck to one, Fitzroy Chapman, head of the Spencer-Chapman family, whose very considerable fortune was derived from their sole concession on the manufacture and importing of sulphuric acid – very unromantic but very welcome. Fitzroy was a good deal older than Audley, in fact he was another of Jim's cronies at Arthur's Club and equally a bon viveur. He was a kind and generous man who sadly in later life became stone deaf so that one had to communicate with him by means of scratch-pads, which he always carried with him as he never learnt to lip-read. Eventually this fearful affliction caused him to lose a good deal of his natural bonhomie and zest for life, and he was apt to relapse into spells of grumpiness when he ignored one's written messages and either mooched off alone to weed in some remote part of his beloved and very beautiful garden or complained about the food and anything else that sprang to mind.

The Chapmans first came into my conscious life when I was taken, at the age of four, to stay in their London house, 4 Hyde Park Square, where I contracted the Spanish 'flu that was then rampaging and killing off so many people. It was a severe bout, I am told, and not helped by the pea-soup fogs that also afflicted us. Certainly I can remember it clearly, and particularly Fitzroy's splendid ear-trumpet. This was on the end of a few feet of flexible tube, like an old-fashioned motor horn and he handed it to me when I was better, hoping I suppose for a charming infantile piping "Good morning". Instead he got an almighty blast from the full force of my recovered lungs which shot him almost out of his chair – a great success I thought, but poor Fitzroy's hearing was not improved. They must have been thoroughly fed up being stuck with obnoxious me and my nanny willie-nillie till I was well enough to travel.

There were three Chapman children: Nell, the same age as Roger with whom when older she ran around for a bit before becoming infatuated with John Gielgud who was then acquiring fame as Hamlet at the Old Vic. She subsequently married another cousin, Sotheby Bird. Next came Stewart, who was my age and a cripple. He had fallen off a wall and dislocated his hip when small, and was so badly treated in costly West End nursing homes that it became tubercular and he ended up with a vast medical boot after years of fearful traction, calipers and torture. He spent many years in a sanatorium in Switzerland but, perhaps unwisely, was allowed to go to Eton which he had always longed to do, but whose Thames-side vapours cannot have done his pulmonary TB much good. Dear Stew was so brave and cheerful, making light of his handicaps, driving fast cars later on (his cousin Glen Kidston of car racing fame being his hero), playing golf and generally living it up as fast as he was able before inevitably dying from a haemorrhage when he was only 23. The third was an afterthought named Pat, who being so much younger did not come much into our lives.

We were often all together up on Deeside and Nell and Stewart occasionally came to stay with us at Southwood, usually when their parents were off in their beautiful pale grey Rolls Royce touring all over the continent and the South of France in particular. Fitzroy's mother was French and I understand he became very Gallic on these trips, bilingual and complete with beret. He loved using the cut-out on the Rolls – a device in the form of a handle protruding through the floorboard between driver and passenger and marked 'For use only on the Continent', which when pulled up allowed the engine to exhaust without benefit of silencers. Thus reducing the exhaust pressure, it provided greater power and speed, with matching deafening noise.

Later visits to the Chapman family are far happier than the Hyde Park Square saga and relate to their country house overlooking the ladies' course at Royal Ashdown. This was close to our prep-school Ashdown House at Forest Row and Audley was very kind taking us to blow-out teas in Eastbourne in her 3½ litre Bentley. You can imagine what a thrill that was for a small boy, whizzing along in those wonderful sports cars with their deep-throated roar, the wind in your hair, holding on tight as Audley, a skilled driver, whisked along at 70mph – very fast for those days. Audley always drove sports cars, played County Golf, was a keen Alpinist and walker in the Cairngorms as well as for some time a regular member of the smart Leicestershire hunts. She was in fact a very racey sort of person and remained extremely active for the whole of her long life, organising walking expeditions and many other outdoor ploys which made her for ever popular with young people. Never a dull moment when Audley was around for she infected everyone with her energy and enthusiasm.

When Jim Thursby-Pelham died the Chapmans inherited his entire collection which, added to Fitzroy's own not inconsiderable antiques, made their house Ashdown Place a veritable feast of goodies which required a procession of experts from the Victoria and Albert Museum, the National Gallery and other institutions to clean, polish and generally preserve. I so well remember the delicious aroma of beeswax, paeonies, azaleas and Havana cigars that pervaded the rooms that housed these treasures.

In our 'teens we spent several Christmases en famille at Ashdown, as members of a large party lavishly entertained in great style with butler, footmen and a host of other staff, plus a chauffeur and five gardeners without. Mills, the butler of very long service, became a lifelong friend and when Pam and I last paid a visit many years later after the war he, as only Mills could with such composure, firmly declined my proffered tip on departure with, "Please not from you, Mr Michael. It's been such a pleasure to see you again, so I hope you will excuse me."

One year, I must have been about 15 at the time, there was a do-it-yourself fancy-dress dinner party on Christmas night to which a few neighbours also came making a large party. It proved a riot. My father shaved off his moustache (the only occasion we ever saw him thus naked), draped himself in sheets and appeared as 'Mother Superior'. He was found by the guests entering the dining-room a little later kneeling before the red velvet curtains with a candelabra on either side gazing Heavenward and offering to hear confessions while telling a string of Audley's pearls. My brother and I had hired wigs from Nathans (a bit of a cheat I suppose), he as Mr Hyde of Jekyll and Hyde, I with a long blonde one as an inadequate representation of Greta Garbo. Roger borrowed an opera cloak which he padded out with newspaper in the shoulders, stuck bits of revolting black hair on his face and hands and at some 6'4" with false fangs was a ghastly sight. He had also stuffed cotton-wool up his nose to dilate his nostrils, an unwise move as you will learn.

I was pinned into an old black velvet dress, suitably padded and décolleté and with false eyelashes and a Garbo mouth plastered onto my still beardless face was pronounced ravishing enough but indifferent as a look-alike.

Aunt Alice as the grandmother of the house was present and had acquired from the old Farquhar dressing-up box a handsome eighteenth century courtier's costume of silk brocade and white satin breeches complete with gold-topped cane and buckled shoes. With her snow-white hair tied back in a black silk moiré bow she looked stunning and damn well knew it. One of the outside guests was a certain divorcée friend of Audley's (who shall be nameless) poured into a clinging dress of gold lamé plunging to cleavage back and front to represent she declared the then topical Gold Standard. She made a great play of 'confessing' to Dad who proved quite ready to oblige. She had plenty to get off her pretty chest as she was at that time trying to winkle the wealthy Fitzroy from her bosom friend.

A high-spot of the evening occurred before dinner when Mills and his minions were handing tray-fuls of White Lady cocktails already poured into Fitzroy's best crystal. Aunt Alice, like all Farquhars a teetotaller, mistook them in the excitement of her success as the courtier for a non-alcoholic beverage and grabbed one from the passing tray. Holding it aloft she cried "Here's tae us whaur's like us" and tossed it back in one. Encouraged by its unexpected warmth no doubt, she completed the performance by hurling the priceless glass into the fireplace and rapidly downed a second. Poor Fitzroy, stone deaf, watched in stark horror and gasping "The bloody woman's mad!" led the party swiftly into dinner to avoid further damage. His by now towering rage evaporated on sighting the Mother Superior as described above with an unctious and repellant smirk on her upturned face.

Nor was Aunt Alice the only one to lose control. Roger never had a strong head for liquor and with his nose bunged up, as I presaged, attained a dangerous flying speed causing him to become really terrifying. Before passing out into the arms of our long-suffering mother, who tucked him safely and without pain back in his bed, he had assaulted Aunt Alice crying that he was about to rape her. I thought he might kill her with fright if nothing worse!

After dinner we played charades, cunningly devised by Reverend Mother, who you will recall was quite a dab hand in this field. The best word we acted was 'circumcise', the final scene of which gave her the chance without too much bother to achieve a sex-change from Abbess to Rabbi. With our luckless cousin Desmond Fitzgerald as victim, and armed with an eight-inch kitchen knife and a concealed carrot, he carried out the operation with panache and a touch too much realism for the weaker members of the audience. It was a splendid climax to a truly memorable evening that can never have been forgotten by anyone present (including the domestic staff I surmise).

You will doubtless have gathered that Aunt Alice was a bossy lady, brimful of self-confidence and often overbearing with a strong inclination to dominate any situation in which she might find herself. She was once in a London cinema when what might have become a dangerous fire was duly announced from the stage by the frightened manager. Nothing daunted, she rose from her stall, brandishing her Brigg's umbrella and crying in a loud voice "Don't panic anyone, just stay calm and remain where you are till I tell you or we shall block all the exits." Such was her power of command that she was instantly and without default obeyed by the stunned audience, permitting her to beat a path with the umbrella to the nearest escape route, on reaching which she turned and told them they might now start evacuating the theatre in an orderly fashion and herself disappeared to safety. She was already well into her eighties.

She attended our wedding in London in 1944 and made her presence felt by talking loudly in church and traversing the ensuing reception proclaiming ecstatically "Michael has married a Botticelli angel". She ended her performance by pinching the sugar submarine that Elsie Surridge, my in-laws' cook and life-long friend, had at great pains procured to top the splendid black market cake she had made for us. Aunt Alice proclaimed that she felt sure we would wish her to have it. Despite her manifold transgressions you had to admire Aunt Alice's nerve and you could not fail to warm to her ebullience and her affectionate nature.

Audley and my father had always been much closer than first cousins – almost brother and sister – and towards the end of her life, after Fitzroy's death, she spent even more time with my parents at Craigveigh. Of course, like all the family, she adored Deeside and walked for miles all over it and the Grampians till the end. So frequently did she stay that one of the spare rooms was always referred to as Audley's room and seldom was anyone else put in it. Indeed, so close was she to my parents and to Andy also that at her express wish she was buried beside them all (and Granny Goodbody) in the St John Great Bed of Ware at St Thomas's church at Aboyne. There they lie with all their varied memories, marked by a row of identical granite crosses. To me a remarkable, diverse and much loved quintet.

Ashdown Place.

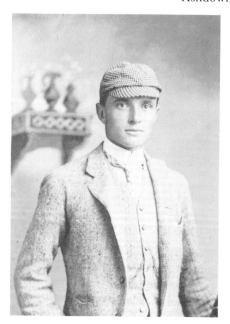

Jim Thursby-Pelham.

Alice Thursby-Pelham.

Part II
DEESIDE SUMMERS

CHAPTER VII

The journey north

I mentioned in chapter three how from the early twenties until the outbreak of World War II we spent our summer holidays with our St John granny, in the midst of a host of her side of our family, the Clan Farquhar.

My earliest recollection of being at Aboyne was with Letty when I must have been about five years old. This memory lingers only because of there being snow on the ground which I had not seen before and of my utter desolation at being left alone with her when my parents took off visiting elsewhere. I was quite sure they were doing a Babes-in-the-Wood act on me. However, these memories properly start in the summer of 1923 after my first term at Ashdown House and cover an uninterrupted succession of school holidays from that year till I went to sea in 1932 and thereafter visits whenever naval service allowed.

Right at the start I recall my schoolboy's mounting excitement as the end of term drew near, anticipating the magic of that enthralling journey on the night train to Aberdeen and the delights towards which it would so swiftly carry me. It rendered the revision for the annual exams, that in the view of authority should have been my main concern, virtually impossible. It kept me awake for many a night, eventually filling my dreams when sheer exhaustion overcame the squirrel-in-a-cage syndrome.

At last, having been collected rather grandly off the school train at

Victoria by Aunt Carrie's Rolls we joined our parents at her town house, 39 Cadogan Place. It is a large Belgravian stucco house on five floors and popular with us as it then had an electric lift and speaking tubes on all floors. It was fortunate that we never broke the lift, travelling up and down, or pushed Aunt Carrie's loyal and devoted cadre of elderly maids beyond endurance by our endless blowing of the speaking tubes' whistles. Luckily, like Aunt Carrie, they loved children and always spoiled us, particularly her lady's maid, Maud Barnes, daughter of a naval family from Gosport who was consequently delighted later with Cadet St John. At the back of the house we could watch Mr Smith's smart livery stables, busy and clattering with the smartest of riders setting forth for Rotten Row.

As a rule, we were posted off till lunch-time to meet our ex-nanny, Letty Hellyer, with her current charges walking in Hyde Park. In the afternoon we enjoyed roaming around nearby Harrods, listening to gramophone records and playing all the Steinways, Bechsteins and Blüthners in the piano department, under the basilisk stare of a frustrated floorwalker. Then, after tea, the portentous start of the Tudor St John caravanserai was signalled by the arrival of not one but two taxis, rendered necessary by the mountain of luggage considered essential in those days. Our school trunks and the family's four bikes had been despatched PLA, so my brother and I had only one Gladstone bag apiece, plus our golf clubs and tennis rackets. Our parents were quite another kettle of fish. They had also sent a trunk PLA from home, but still had with them three large leather suitcases, two fitted dressing cases, three attaché cases, two hat-boxes, two sets of golf clubs, a picnic basket and to round it off, a hefty hold-all carrying many spare pillows (my 'trachy' father had to sleep always in a sitting position), plus umbrellas and walking-sticks.

This vast collection was counted into and out of the taxis, ending up on a large trolley at the station where my father, with all the aura of military authority and the precision attributable to a QMG, supervised its labelling and placing into one of the several luggage-vans attached to our already lengthy night express. For handling this load, our porter accepted with genuine gratitude a tip of half-a-crown (12½p today).

According to the whim of my parents we travelled either on the LNER east coast route *Aberdonian* from Kings Cross or the LMS's equally prestigious *Highlander* from Euston over Shap Fell on the west. Both trains then sparkled in their distinctive liveries and I seem to recall comprised as many as 19 carriages, hauled by two magnificent steam locomotives, green Pacific class on the LNER and rich, gleaming red on the LMS. They were beautiful and enthralling to schoolboys and my heart beat fast as I walked their length before climbing into my third class sleeper.

Each train had a dining-car on the end to be dropped off, after serving two five-course dinners, at either York or Crewe. They were profusely decked with mahogany and satin-wood marquetry, pink silk shaded lamps, damask table-cloths and plush-covered chairs – and the food was good too! Having rushed to book tickets for the first service you got into the diner before departure but had to struggle with the train at high speed up the many swaying carriages after your meal. The luggage-vans and the guard's van were redolent with the smell of fish-curing, and usually there were rather forlorn gun-dogs chained up on sacks in the corner that needed patting as you passed.

It was always a pleasurable trauma to transfer one's allegiance from one train to the other, akin to the impossible task of shifting loyalties from Oxford to Cambridge for the boat-race.

I never managed to sleep before we lost our dining-car, but instead spent a happy hour gazing out of the window and drinking in the thrill and sense of adventure of the speed, dashing full tilt through the night with the rush of passing lights, the whoosh of bridges, and the roar and rattle of our progress. The two main lines met next morning at a junction just north of Montrose before completing the final impressive scenic stretch up the North Sea coast of Angus to Aberdeen. As both expresses were due at this junction within minutes of each other, there was always a race to reach it ahead of one's rival and be first into the station buffet for a good, fat Scottish breakfast of porridge, baps and Finnan haddock with poached eggs. Consequently we were up and alert with excitement by either Dundee or Perth, waiting to see if we had won, and so too were many of our fellow passengers. Being first also carried the added bonus for me of being able to watch the other train led in by the clanking, hissing pair of gleaming engines, with their smell of hot oil and their escaping steam, gliding past to a graceful halt round the long, curved platform.

Breakfast over, we sallied forth again into the crystal clear, champagne air that keeps the locals alive to great ages, and into the little Deeside train, the QMG having once more successfully conducted the logistic exercise of transferring the luggage mountain from the London train. This locally renowned train now puffed us up the River Dee, with frequent stops at a succession of neat timber or granite stations over what was held to be the best kept and most scenic stretch of line in the British Isles. Doubtless this can be attributed not only to the beauties of the Dee Valley up which it wended its way to the terminus at Ballater, but also to the fact that it owed its existence to Queen Victoria's travelling over it in the royal train to her beloved Balmoral, a practice duly followed by her descendants year after year.

Alas, these railway glories are long since gone, the polished and colourful steam locomotives giving way to dirty, grime-laden diesels; the carriages no longer bright and shining in their distinctive liveries, but tricked out in an anonymous, tepid blue and white, scarcely visible beneath the dirt that is today seldom cleaned off. The spotless and varied décor of the first class sleepers has given way to plastic and formica – well scratched with the graffiti of football drunks and the like and you cannot see out of the windows for filth.

The restaurant cars have disappeared and so, finally, has the Deeside line, ripped untimely from its heather bed by Dr Beeching and now barely discernible beneath the invading scrub, its vandalised stations staring blindly out of the ruins through boarded windows. The west coast route now goes no further than Perth, so the races and the rivalry are no more, and anyway, you can count yourself extremely lucky if the *Aberdonian* arrives less than an hour late. Nobody seems to care: Pride died with nationalisation.

Now, as I write, I am pleased to say there are faint signs at last of efforts to improve this run-down wreck of past glories – even talk of electrifying the east coast route. But I note that the new sleepers have been designed for dwarfs and should you light a cigarette the smoke alarm in your berth brings the train to a grinding – and prolonged – halt.

I make no apology for this digression on the railways for to a small boy, and indeed many adults also, the glories of the steam railways of the country before nationalisation can never be forgotten by us who were alive to enjoy them and difficult, I think, for those born too late to begin even dimly to appreciate.

Not long after the acquisition of the car that I described in chapter three, and when my parents reckoned they were experienced enough in its safe conduct, we made the first adventurous journey by road from Oxfordshire to Deeside in that faithful old Wolseley. The journey was carefully planned by my father, as if he were Wellington advancing across the Iberian Peninsula, in stages of around 150 to 200 miles – never more, and a decent stint at that for one driver (my mother till we boys were old enough to help). The twisting roads and busy towns through which we passed, there being few if any bypasses and no dual carriageways at all, combined to keep one's average speed well below 30 mph. The car's maximum speed was 50 mph down wind, and the slightest hill required a difficult and very physical gear-change. The greater part of the luggage mountain had been sent ahead by rail, leaving the grid at the rear of the car carrying four heavy suitcases that created a dangerous tendency for you to lose your back-end on badly cambered corners. Our capacious, well-stocked picnic basket travelled between my brother and myself on the back seat. With four St Johns each weighing in at anything from 10 to 16 stone, it needed every foot-pound of the 15 horses to get us north, but we never broke down or even had a puncture – thank God!

The schedule was tailored to various family or friends' residences where we stayed for the night, sometimes two nights, leaving after breakfast with the picnic basket lavishly replenished by our more than kind hosts. Our journey was early dubbed 'The St John spongeing tour', but in fairness it must be said that the hosts were never in the least unwilling and without exception were regular visitors at the Old Mill House and later at Southwood. Our welcomes were unfailingly warm.

The first stage was always via Oxford, Banbury and Rugby to just north of Leicester – a terrible town to get through – to Rothley Temple, stately Elizabethan home of Ernie and Katie Broadhurst (of Tootal Broadhurst, the cotton manufacturers). He was a polio victim who could walk only with great difficulty on two sticks indoors and out of doors propelled himself in a very swish bathchair. Katie was a Scotswoman from Aberdeenshire, so they spent quite a time each summer at the Huntly Arms Hotel in Aboyne.

On leaving Rothley, the first part of our route lay along the Fosse Way – dead straight and switchbacked for many miles – and it was here that on one occasion, breasting the brow of a hill with a fine following wind, we ran without warning into a long stretch of wet tar on a steepish downward slope. I have to say that 50 or more years later I can vividly recall my mother's frantic wrestling with the direct-drive steering-wheel over her ample bosom, my father's rigid terror in the front seat, with hands over his head and feet pushing through the floorboards, the astonished faces of the road-workers leaping for safety as we rocketed spiralling by, and my brother and I in stitches at the back, enjoying every foolhardy moment without a trace of fear.

Thanks to Providence and my mother's strong instinct for survival, we came to rest unharmed in the valley. Whereupon as a reaction from his terror, my father, an appalling car-passenger in all circumstances, let fly a volley of pent-up abuse and a fine row to the delight of the back seat audience ensued, ending in his being told "he could bloody well drive himself, she was fed up with it". It was then our turn for terror, for he had not driven anything since before the 1914/18 War. However as the road in those days was virtually deserted, and there being no corners on a Roman road, we survived a mile or so of erratic, impulsive progress before both parents suddenly saw the joke, hysterics broke out and peace and matriarchal safe conduct were restored.

Lunch on this second leg was always in the Dukeries, just past the vast gates of, I think, the Duke of Portland's place, after which we either went via Newark to Lincoln to stay with Bishop Swaine and his wife Angie in the palace, or up the A1 to Morpeth to visit my father's old comrade-in-arms in 'The Fifth', Ben Cruddas and his Harmsworth wife Dodder with their large family.

Angie Swaine was a Farquharson and so she and The Bish always took lodgings for August in Aboyne, where they were very much part of the social scene, playing golf and joining many picnics and parties. Staying in the palace, vast, echoing and replete with batchelor chambers for the ordinands where Roger and I slept, entailed attending His Grace's morning prayers in the private chapel. Here the St John family sat in the choir, confronted by the usual prayer desk. It transpired that this was not fixed to the floor, and since it was designed for choirboys, became instantly unstable under the combined assault of four hefty, and taller bodies descending on it to pray. On the first occasion our forward momentum simply carried us straight on over the top and we ended in a deafening crash prostrate across the chancel on our faces at the Bishop's feet with the prayer desk beneath us. Of course, everyone, and most of all the Bish and Angie, had to burst out laughing, the odour of sanctity having evaporated in an instant. Five or so minutes later, with us restored after a difficult struggle to the kneeling position, prayers were with difficulty swiftly concluded.

I remember I excelled myself at Lincoln by writing my roofer in a spare moment on Palace notepaper before we left, so as to get this boring chore out of the way, and it greatly diverted the Swaines to receive a letter under their own letterhead.

Stage three was occasionally over Carter Bar from the Cruddas's but usually via Scotch Corner and over Bowes Moor to Carlisle. My mother always became excited about sighting Skiddaw or Scaw Fell and had her leg pulled by false alarms from us. Very occasionally we came by the western road over Shap which tested the Wolseley severely and required stops for topping up the radiator.

Once in Scotland, the next visit was either with spinster sisters called Ballard (old friends from Limerick) in Dumfriesshire or Uncle Edmund St John and Aunt Di near Edinburgh.

The final stage was naturally the most exciting. Another long climb over Beattoch and a dreary succession of mining towns brought us at last through Stirling into Perthshire and our first glimpse of the Highland Hills to the north across Allen water. Lunch on this stage was always sitting on the same stone dyke, sheltered by fir trees, somewhere beyond

Auchterarder. We became so attached to all these picnic spots that we used the same ones on our journeys south. At Perth we had the choice of tackling the Spittal of Glenshee road to Braemar or less frequently, if our nerve failed, the longer but less precipitous route via Brechin over the Cairn-o-Mount to Strachan.

The Spittal road, in those days, was for much of its length either single track or only wide enough for two cars to pass with great care, switchbacked and unfenced against wandering sheep. It wound for miles up the glen to the notorious one-in-three hairpin bend aptly named 'The Devil's Elbow'. Driving the old Wolseley up this formidable obstacle was a hairy and thrilling business; the gear-shift was so stiff you could not risk going straight at the Elbow. The technique was to stop some way below where the gradient was comparatively less severe and get into bottom gear, attacking the double hairpin in one suspense-laden high-revving noisy grind. We all held our breath and let out a great cheer of relief as we reached the top without disaster. This constituted the crowning achievement of the entire journey and led on to the quiet downhill coast to Braemar and the River Dee. The scenery became increasingly beautiful, the old car seemed to gather strength and we ourselves to rise to the very peak of enjoyment and high spirits as we bowled down Deeside, every inch of which we knew and loved so well.

Now, of course, one thinks nothing of driving the motorways from Sussex to Aberdeenshire in a day, buffeting your fume-ridden way on dual carriageways over the graded and straightened Shap Fell and Beattoch; the Devil's Elbow itself has disappeared and the Spittal of Glenshee now widened and re-graded to take the ski-parties to the summit. It is not safe to spare a glance at the countryside now for the need you have to concentrate on avoiding death on our overcrowded roads.

The Bish and Angie Swain on the Cairn-o-Mount

Drumnagesk c. 1900. Standing: Jim Farquhar, Dick St John, Tudor St John, Hobart Farquhar, Bertie Farquhar and Charlie Farquhar. Sitting: Mowbray Farquhar, Marion Farquhar, Addie St John, Sir Arthur Farquhar, Janie Farquhar and Billie Farquhar

CHAPTER VIII
The clan 'greats'

1. A CATALOGUE OF THE FARQUHARS
OF DRUMNAGESK

To write about our holidays in Scotland without first telling my readers of whom the Farquhar Clan consisted would be attempting Hamlet without the Prince of Denmark, for in their individual ways they were all very much part of the scene, our lives closely involved in their activities and our quieter moments greatly enlivened by tales of their often remarkable occasions. So please bear with me while I introduce them.

My great-great-grandfather was Admiral Sir Arthur Farquhar KCB, who made history during the Napoleonic Wars in command of the frigate *Acheron*, successfully fighting the first recorded convoy protection action off the east coast of America. His eldest son, my great-grandfather, became in due course the second Admiral Sir Arthur Farquhar KCB before retiring to Drumnagesk with his baker's dozen of surviving children, my great-aunts and great-uncles (the Lord knows how many misses there might have been). One of them became the third Admiral Sir Arthur Farquhar KCB in direct succession. Two other sons also made it to flag rank and it is thus not surprising that the family's naval tradition was sustained long enough to engulf me two generations later.

All but two of these 13 great-relations survived into their eighties and two managed to last into their ninth decade. This was, in their day, a remarkable actuarial achievement, though perhaps not so striking in the

1980s. It prompts me to mention again the comparative longevity of the inhabitants of the north east of Scotland, with its clean, clear champagne air and tough winters, that continues to be evident to this day.

There were four girls: Kinty, the eldest, who married a distinguished Cambridge don named Caldwell and died giving birth to my cousin Keith; Janie, who remained a spinster and became the family's sad drudge; Adeline (Addie) my grandmother; and Alice who featured in chapter four, the London butterfly of the naughty '90s, who married the rich and charming dilettante Jim Thursby-Pelham.

The nine boys were Jimsy, who finally settled in Vancouver (a nonagenarian); Arthur, the Admiral; Bill, a great bon viveur and raconteur, who became a sort of social secretary or court jester to John D Rockefeller no less, and married a Chicago meat heiress; Mowbray, a soldier who later joined BSA and patented the Farquhar Rifle that lost out to the short Lee-Enfield; Dick, another Admiral; Hubbard, who was killed in the 1914/18 war; Charlie, who was Chief Commissioner of Police in the Punjab; Stuart, the third Admiral; and Alice's twin brother Bertie, who having been badly gassed in the 1914/18 war failed to make 80. Bertie was, you will recall, involved in the dramas of my mother's visit to Boulogne.

I gather they all grew up pretty wild at Drumnagesk, the boys becoming skillful poachers from an early age. As a result they were without exception already excellent shots and successful fishermen before they were fully grown. By the time we came to know them their reputation was firmly established as the most varied, fascinating and gregarious bunch of people that one could imagine. With the exception of Jim in Canada who seldom visited the UK the eleven survivors continued to haunt Deeside at every available opportunity and four of them lived in Aboyne, following the eventual sale of Drumnagesk. None of them smoked or drank, but held no overbearing opinions concerning those who did. They possessed remarkably fine speaking voices and read aloud beautifully, in particular the lessons in church. The males could also make themselves heard effortlessly over great distances when required — and their roaring on the golf-course and elsewhere would have out-decibelled even Charles St John's Muckle Hart of Benmore.

Another clan gathering at Drumnagesk with my St John Grandmother on the extreme right and my Farquhar Great Grandparents seated beside her

The Farquhars never possessed any shooting or fishing rights and, with few minor exceptions, neglected to rent any. They simply did not need to since they were constantly in demand as shooting or fishing guests of their neighbouring lairds who, being anxious to swell the bag and enliven their house-parties, were delighted to have the Farquhar skill on moor or river and their gregarious presence to help entertain their house-parties.

It was a token of their widespread popularity that they were always referred to as Uncle This or Aunt That. A laird would say he was inviting Uncle Arthur or Uncle Charlie to shoot and his wife that she was asking Aunt Addie to tea. The only exception to this was Uncle Arthur's wife, my Great-Aunt Eve, who was of course Mother Eve without fail.

The male Farquhars strictly observed their own self-made rule in life that an invitation to shoot or fish took automatic precedence over all other social engagements, weddings and funerals included, and the lady Farquhars, strong characters though they for the most part were, had to accept it come what might.

2. THE ABOYNE QUARTET

Our lack of grandfathers was for us amply compensated for by our good fortune in having not only such a splendid Granny Goodbody, but equally a Gan-Gan St John, the first of the four Farquhars to move to Aboyne, of whom also we were very fond and who was unfailingly kind to us. Happily they were as different as chalk from cheese; the one as already described, quiet and retiring, while Gan-Gan was forever in the forefront of the family affairs and the County. As the Honourable Mrs E T St John, daughter-in-law of the fourteenth Baron, she named her house Bletsoe, lest anyone be tempted to overlook her status, but I have to say that this little affectation apart, she was no snob.

The Bletsoe we knew was the second of that ilk in the village into which Gan-Gan had moved to share house with my Uncle Andy. It stands beside the spacious village green, called for some reason 'The Charlestown of Aboyne', opposite the old school buildings. It was two semis knocked into one and consequently full of awkward, crooked passages and open spaces in the wrong place, but it was a very happy second home for us all. In those days it was staffed by three loyal retainers who, in the nature of things, were Roger's and my close friends and allies, and of whom I will have more to tell later.

Uncle Andy, Gan-Gan's third son, having with his youngest brother Dick been a victim of the notorious 'Geddes Axe' after the 1914/18 war, joined his mother on his Naval Commander's retired pay to augment the meagre competence he had inherited through his long-dead parson father and for the remainder of his 85 years never did another stroke of work. He was by far my favourite uncle, as well as my very generous godfather, and he was the closest of his brothers to my father and ourselves. He had a delightfully mordant wit and was remarkably well-read, particularly in Greek and Roman mythology which he often related with comic effect to events and people surrounding him.

Sadly he remained a batchelor, infatuated over the years by a very beautiful, but entirely unscrupulous widow who flagrantly abused his devotion to her and was consequently loathed but endured by us, together with her spoilt and unpleasant only daughter. You will recall it was she who featured in the *Killing of Sister George* incident. As I remember him now, so many years later, I realise that Andy must have always been a sad man, longing I suspect for the family and home of his own which fate decreed would never be his. If so, he never showed any outward sign of sadness, but always applied himself to getting the best out of everyone and everything that came his way, particularly his four nephews and one niece. He was thus a very popular member of his generation, known always in the village, where he was frequently to be seen shopping in his lovat green plus-fours and heavy fell-walking turned-up black brogues, as The Commander – for them there was no other of that rank. Like his Farquhar uncles, he also never lacked invitations to fish and shoot all over the county. As I shall later relate, he was also an eccentric and diverting golfer, but just now I will conclude this brief introduction of Bletsoe's master by saying that I could not possibly have been fonder of anyone than I was of my Uncle Andy and I have his medals mounted over my bed to remind me of countless happy occasions.

Craigevar Castle

Inneshewen. From left to right: Andy St. John, Bill Farquhar, Had Peck, Marion Farquhar with Jean Farquhar, Tudor St John, Jo Peck and Anna Peck

Close by up the Brae behind Bletsoe lived the Admiral, Uncle Arthur, with Aunt Eve in the house they not surprisingly called 'Acheron' where he installed a smart white flagstaff on which he flew the white ensign – quite incorrectly and unentitled – on every conceivable occasion. They also owned a house on the west coast outside Oban, inherited from Aunt Eve's family, the McNeils, in which they wintered in the softer climate of Argyll.

Uncle Arthur could have been the model for a Bateman Admiral; short and stocky with somewhat simean arms hanging from broad shoulders on which his large, round head rested, thrust forward without it seemed benefit of a neck. Tufts of white cotton-wool sprouted from his ears and nostrils, showing up vividly against his round, ruddy complexion. His face was perpetually creased in smiles causing his bright brown eyes to disappear completely. All was topped with the Farquhar silver hair, though his was, by the '20s, balding and his bare dome splashed with large brown freckles. He was a sharp dresser, particularly in highland regalia, possessing a number of different Farquhar tartan kilts – hunting, dress, ancient, natural dye and so on across the spectrum dreamt up by the Scottish wool weavers to boost business. In daytime these were worn with a sponge-bag coat and waistcoat and a matching Balmoral bonnet that caused him to resemble somewhat his close acquaintance Sir Harry Lauder.

Aunt Eve was a stately, fading red-haired scion of her Clan and a tremendous snob who, as Lady Farquhar, had early established her precedence as wife of the head of the family in the absence of Jim in Canada. (I should explain here in parentheses that in this particular she had a worthy and successful rival in the Honourable Mrs E T St John of Bletsoe; I think it fair to say they shared the honours of the social scene equally, and thank Heaven without trace of rancour. In fact, more often than not they were staunch allies whom it would have been unthinkable to hinder or oppose in the slightest way.)

Each year Aunt Eve hauled Uncle Arthur in state to Balmoral to sign the royal visitors' book and so ensure an invitation to the garden party. At the height of the Deeside season, she gave an immense Tea Party (note my capital letters) for which she hired the Victory Hall in

Great Grandfather Farquhar with his Grandsons.
Standing: Dick St John, Alaistair Farquhar, Keith Caldwell and Andy St John.
Seated: Tudor St John with Tom Farquhar, The Admiral with John Farquhar
and Edmund St John with Malcolm Farquhar

Great Grandmother Farquhar with her Grand-daughters. Standing: Nina Farquhar, Nellie Farquhar and Mollie Farquhar. Seated: Dee Farquhar, Audley Thursby-Pelham, Lady Farquhar and Dolly Thursby-Pelham

Uncle Bill tells yet another story to my parents – Aunt Carrie in the background. 1937

Myself fishing The Long Haugh at Dess. 1935

Aboyne and invited the entire Quality of at least three counties. It was equalled only by Annie Cowdray's vast annual Thé Dansant at Dunecht and indeed could perhaps have been considered a sort of riposte to the, in her estimation, arriviste pretensions of Wheatman Pearson's widow.

Aunt Eve can best be described as the poor man's Queen Mary, with her all-pervading concern for decorum and her well-sustained performance as the matriarch. As I've said, she was 'Mother Eve' to one and all who held her in great affection. For she was amongst the kindest, wisest and most gregarious of women and although many of her tenets were thoroughly outdated, as for instance her disdain acquired in the days of sail for Royal Marines or NOs of other than 'Executive' rank, one could easily forgive them in such a friendly, honest soul. She was appalled to learn that I had joined the Submarine Service in 1936, where battle ensigns could not be flown when engaging the enemy more closely and I was only restored to grace when she heard that it was at Their Lordships' command and not as a volunteer that this transfer to a private navy had occurred.

That Aunt Eve was a remarkably brave woman was demonstrated to the county at large when Uncle Arthur, in his late seventies, decided to buy a car and, never having driven in his life and after only the most rudimentary instruction from the man who delivered it, climbed behind the wheel and started a personal reign of terror on the Deeside roads. It was an open four-seater Citroën, with central gear-shift and hand-brake and a bulb horn mounted high on the off-side of the windscreen. It was bright red, some said unkindly like the scuppers of Britain's wooden walls to hide the blood. Uncle Arthur's technique on approaching a corner was first to disengage the gears and coast towards the hazard, arresting his progress in spasms by applying the hand-brake in a succession of jerks with his left hand (pony-traps lacked foot-brakes, so for some time he had no notion of their use). Nearer to the corner, his right hand also came off the wheel in order to send forth a series of blasts on the bulb horn, approximating as nearly as he could manage to the signals laid down in the Board of Trade's *International Rules for the Safety of Life at Sea*; for example, four short blasts meant "Keep out of my way – I cannot keep out of yours"! Appropriate you might say in a car that was steering itself. This hairy process his long-suffering Lady endured without the flicker of an eyelid for several years until, from bitter experience, he acquired a slightly better understanding of modern road transport. In the meantime, any advice from kind friends was met by a salvo of scornful indignation, "If I could command a squadron of battleships, what makes you think I can't manage this damn thing?"

At the foot of the brae, across the road from Bletsoe, Aunt Janie the spinster lived in a neat little semi-detached villa, under the stern eye of my grandmother and the very necessary protection of Uncle Andy. She was now a frail, rheumy little lady with a quavering, high-pitched voice and watery pale blue eyes, treated all her life by her brothers and sisters as a half-wit and referred to by all as Poor Janie. From her earliest years it is evident that she was the butt of all the vast Farquhar family's less admirable traits and, after old Lady Farquhar's demise, became the Drumnagesk drudge under the imperious rule of my grandmother, who in my day still lost patience with her sister, berating her with "Don't be a fool, Janie" whenever their paths crossed.

One of Aunt Janie's chores in the old days was the care of the Drumnagesk chickens which free-ranged round the policies, sometimes roosting in the Scotch firs. She never understood why, when she was feeding them, they would on occasions fall out of the trees dead at her feet, causing her to squeak loudly. I am ashamed to record that the cause was my father who, together with his two younger brothers, Andy and Dick, was picking them off with an airgun from the shelter of the nearby rhododendrons.

The old Admiral and Lady Farquhar frequently threw large dinner parties for 20 or more people at Drumnagesk. It is related that on one occasion Aunt Janie, then well into her fifties, was so startled at being addressed suddenly by the man next to her that she spilt all her soup, whereupon the old Admiral roared from the head of the table, "Janie, you're a disgrace – you don't know how to behave . . . Go to bed at once" – and so poor Janie meekly did, in front of all that company and worse still the servants.

In her capacity as a drudge, she was at one time shipped off to keep house for her brothers Jim and Bill on a ranch in Canada, but was able to

The four St John brothers. Andy, Edmund, Tudor and Dick, 1937

A naval occasion at Drumnagesk with The Old Admiral aged 90. c. 1905

escape that slavery and return to Deeside before many years when the place was sold and they went their several ways.

One holiday she caused a great tamasha. It was her habit to go by train to the chiropodist in Aberdeen and on this occasion was dozing quietly on the return journey, waking only as the train was pulling out of Aboyne and about to disappear into the long tunnel beneath the village. She screamed and waved her Sary Gamp umbrella frantically out of the window as she disappeared in a cloud of steam into the Stygian depths. Roaring with laughter, the stationmaster at once phoned The Commander to report urgently that "Miss Farquhar's (pronounced in Scotland "Farker's") been carried past Aboyne" and poor Andy had to get his old BSA banger out and drive up the glen to Dinnet, the next stop, where the staff had been alerted to retrieve her.

We were rightly encouraged by our parents to pay Aunt Janie a visit at least once during the holidays, and to bid her goodbye before travelling south to school when she would tip us half-a-crown each, a considerable sum for her. She seemed to me like one of Beatrix Potter's retiring little fieldmice, sitting so quietly in her small front room full of ornaments and treasured bits and pieces from her Victorian past. I found her sweetly gentle and infinitely sad, full of much kindness that she found difficulty in expressing – to schoolboys anyway. But gentle kindness was there all right – Poor Janie, she crept mouselike into her nineties in the end.

The fourth Farquhar to settle in Aboyne was the ex-Chief Commissioner of Indian Police in the Punjab Uncle Charlie, and his majestic mem-sahib Aunt Dorothy, whom he had met and married as little Dot Stanier, the toast of the regiment many years earlier. They had bought a large, dark, Victorian villa called Craiglarach across the bridge on the south side of the Dee. It was surrounded by a veranda supported on the highly varnished, rustic fir trunks that were beloved of that era and with a gloomy pine-clad interior that made an incongruous setting for the accumulated Benares brass, Baluchi helmets, carved sandalwood screens, charpoys and other clutter collected during their long sojourn in the Subcontinent. There was one outstanding feature of local colour to offset this oriental plethora. It was an ancient stuffed capercailzie, which hung with outspread wings on a long wire in the well of the staircase where it revolved slowly and relentlessly, first one way, then the other, collecting the dust of ages and home, no doubt, to generations of moths.

Although we could appreciate that Aunt Dorothy had once been a great beauty for she still had very handsome features with a noble Roman nose and a stately deportment, the years of heat and dust had seared her skin and tragically promoted a wiry growth of ginger moustache and beard that rendered dutiful salutes an agony for little boys. My father related that on first returning to Aboyne, Aunt Dorothy, an imposing patrician figure, promenaded to church in a white tussore coat and skirt of antique cut, double-terrai hat with a veil and carrying a green-lined white silk parasol. If true, it was surely a rivetting spectacle amongst the tweeds and tartans of the Highland season; but here I am obliged to confess that my father loved to embroider a good tale and doubtless this delightful recollection might be among the more apochryphal.

Uncle Charlie was well endowed with the family's good looks and verve. Being one of the younger greats, he was still active enough for tennis which, like most kwa-hais he played well. Having his own hard court he threw frequent well-run tennis parties, of far better than vicarage standard, which we all much enjoyed. This did not, of course, interfere with his shooting or fishing. He was also a regular reader of the first lesson in St Thomas's Episcopal Church to such telling effect that a member of the congregation was once heard to remark that he thought it *was* the prophet Isaiah speaking.

Aunt Dorothy, despite their being quite comfortably off and quite out of character with her normally generous nature, had developed a mania for economy in housekeeping with dire results for her long suffering family and guests. Two examples will suffice to show the catastrophic dimensions of the resulting privation. At dinner, when my parents were staying at Craiglarach (as they usually did after the school holidays were over, my father enjoying the House of Commons endless summer recess from mid-July to late October), the menu was oxtail soup, oxtail stew and marrow bones for a savoury. Uncle Charlie roared in fury for the cold beef to be brought in, Aunt Dorothy retired in tears and, or so my father claimed, having had a go at the beef my mother, whose appetite was justly famed, filched a handful of biscuits from the dog's bowl at the foot of the stairs on her way to bed.

The proper owner of this bowl was a large golden retriever bitch called Storm who features in my second example. My father and Aunt Dorothy had taken her for a walk up the farm lanes behind the house and before they had gone far Storm came back in triumph with a leveret, which she surrendered in best field-trial fashion to Aunt Dorothy. Having dispatched this trophy with a mighty blow of her Malacca cane, Aunt Dorothy walked on, swinging the meagre corpse in her left hand, until they came upon a turnip (local term 'neep') that had fallen onto the road off a farm cart. This was also retrieved and she stood pensively studying her trophies. After a long pause she remarked, "I might ask the Farquharsons of Allargue to lunch next Sunday" – and she did.

She had a robust personality, and Charlie and her children had their work cut out to keep abreast of her. She loved to tell long, rambling stories in her slow, rich, contralto voice, delivered it seemed from the bridge of her nose, that really had no point and taken on their own were utterly boring. As told by her however, they became a sort of cabaret turn, bearable in small doses as on the occasion when staying with us at Henley. She related how she was to catch the mail train from Lucknow to 'Pindi with Charlie's parrot in its cage, and her subterfuge to get it unlawfully into her compartment: "So I stopped the tong*ah* in the Ba*zah* and bought a bunch of banān*ahs*. Then I just hid Polly's cage between my legs under my skirt and fed her banān*ahs* all the way to 'Pindi to keep her quiet." The vision this conjured up in the assembled vulgar minds of the Tudor St Johns caused chaos at dinner table and our nice parlour-maid Mary was rivetted to the carpet holding a casserole, rigid, wide-eyed and puce from suppressed giggles. Aunt Dorothy was delighted with her success but quite unaware of its true cause.

Inneshewen, 1938. The last great gathering of the Clan

CHAPTER IX

The rest of the 'greats'

Having described the four Farquhars living in Aboyne, I will now tell you more about the others, starting with brother number three, Great Uncle Bill. He and Marian (née Peck) his American wife had brought her three sisters over from Chicago, all of whom stayed in this country. Anna the eldest, remained a spinster and bred chow-dogs that she came closely to resemble in her house on the Sunningdale side of Chobham. Haraldine (Had for short), who once had a shine for my father and subsequently became my godmother, married a man called Legge and the youngest and prettiest, Jo, married a naughty fellow in the brigade named Whitbread. They were all to be seen from time to time on Deeside and they regularly visited us in the South.

As well as his infectious bonhomie and skill as a raconteur, Uncle Bill was, as I have mentioned, a notable bon viveur and gourmand; he was one of the greediest eaters I have ever come across and his table manners were atrocious – utterly Rabelaisian in fact. It is a measure of his wit and charm that this defect was always overlooked by the host of people happy to entertain him.

He was particularly a master of the Doric story, with his authentic Aberdonian brogue as well as American negro stories learnt during his time with the Rockefellers. When he died I was left a cigarette case inscribed "Bill, from the Lunch-bunch"; whether they met at the Algonquin or the New York Metropolitan Club I never discovered, but I believe he frequented both in his day. Wherever he went he invoked laughter and merriment with his unquenchable high spririts and bottomless fund of reminiscences and tales. For some strange reason one of his parlour-tricks was to recite at speed, and word-perfectly, Oscar Wilde's *Ballad of Reading Gaol* to which his audiences listened spellbound – God alone knows why. It follows that with his immense greed he was the roly-poly Farquhar, agile enough but his Albert spanned a goodly girth. He sported a well-kept walrus moustache and invariably wore a grey Edwardian homburg hat of goodly vintage, with the bow at the back.

The best instance of Billy's exuberance in my ken occurred at Gan-Gan's funeral at Kincardine-O'Niel. The local custom was followed whereby eight of the deceased's closest relations or friends each hold a rope with which together they lower the coffin into its grave and Billy was one of the team. There was a bunch of malmaison carnations on her coffin being buried with her – a last tribute from her four sons – seeing which Billy bent over and picked one, putting it in his button-hole and remarking, as he helped to lower his sister to her final resting-place, "Nice flowers – pity to waste them all and I'm sure Addie would agree" The funeral over, he commented as he walked away with his elder brother Arthur the Admiral, a notorious hypochondriac, "Well Arthur there goes Addie – we're all going off now like chestnuts in front of the fire!"; whereupon it is said Uncle Arthur rushed back to Acheron to put on another woollie and took his temperature. It was all typical Uncle Bill stuff and far from giving any offence, served to cheer up the party and make everyone feel better, as Gan-Gan indeed would have wished. Doubtless she was laughing on cloud nine.

Billy and Marian were, I am glad to say, regular summer visitors to Aboyne with their only daughter Jean, for they contributed much to the goings-on, despite his no longer shooting, fishing or playing golf. The likes of me would have been a deal the poorer if we had missed their enlivening company.

The next brother was the second Admiral, Richard, always known as Dick, likewise a regular visitor with his family to Aboyne where he eventually settled and died. Uncle Dick was an intellectual, smallish and very dapper naval man, with a closely trimmed white imperial and shortish silver hair parted in the centre. He was a gentle person with a quiet but telling manner and a soft voice. He had had a brilliant naval career as one of the brains that hauled the service out of its wooden walls, canvas and broadsides fired at point-blank range into the modern era of steel, steam and accurate long-range weaponry; in all of which he was a close associate of inter alia the great Jackie Fisher. Alas, early in life as a Sub-Lieutenant in the Mediterranean, he met and was hooked for life by a formidable female named Mary, of uncertain origin – some say Cypriot but I have never discovered the truth – who swiftly became notorious throughout the fleet. It is said that eventually she was instrumental in putting an end to Uncle Dick's promising career by being so impossibly rude and unpleasant to the Royals who were making a progress in his flagship. Anyway, shortly after that cruise he retired to Southsea as a Vice Admiral with a CB and little on which to support her and their three daughters. She was generally known by one and all as Black Maria.

By the time they had retired to Aboyne in the 1940s, Aunt Maria's sight was failing, though not nearly so seriously as she chose to make out, and she made Uncle Dick, by then well into his eighties, tow her about the village for all to see with the belt of his mackintosh tied round his neck and shoulder like a guide dog. As everyone without exception could not help being very fond of Uncle Dick, this display served to set the seal finally upon her universal unpopularity and there were, therefore, no regrets when she finally managed to do the only right thing in her life by predeceasing her older spouse; leaving him happily to enjoy, as it turned out, quite a few untrammelled twilight years.

It was in 1944, during this last serene period of his life, that dear old Uncle Dick, who was then lodging at Bletsoe, walked up the Brae to my parents' house to greet my fiancée Pam, jumping over the low granite parapet in the front to present her with a sprig of white heather that he had found out walking the moors and saluting her with a smacking kiss – she was enchanted!

I was helping to fight the war in the Med when Aunt Maria went, but I received a classic account of her obsequies in a letter from my father, which I stupidly lost; in fact, I have none of his letters and bitterly regret not having kept them for he was an engaging and witty correspondent. I remember he started this letter: "Black Maria's gone below; praise God from whom all blessings flow. She died last Friday and they burnt her on Tuesday in case there'd been a mistake!" He went on to relate how for a start she had been included among the last victims of one of Aberdeen's most senior citizens as owner of the crematorium. He was earning a fortune flogging the coffin lids to a local firm who were making wooden cabinets for wartime utility wireless sets; while his brother-in-law, the accredited florist, was equally getting rich reprocessing the floral tributes from one funeral to the next simply by changing the cards, thereby getting paid eight times for one consignment each day. They both ended up in Peterhead gaol for a goodly stretch shortly afterwards.

This was just the start of the saga; worse was to follow as she had deposed that half her ashes were to be buried with Uncle Dick in the Lair which like all good Episcopaleans they had reserved in St Thomas's churchyard at Aboyne, and the remainder scattered over the summit of a neighbouring hill called Craig-an-Dhinnie. The reigning piscy rector of St Thomas's was one George Martineau. He was in his forties but, having been victim in childhood to drastic rheumatic fever, was left a very delicate man, unfit for war service. He and his wife, Christian, were a charming, amusing pair with four delightful children, but George had one shortcoming: a bad memory coupled with an engaging, unflappable vagueness, being it seemed forever floating on some higher plane.

So it was that on the cold, wet, windy November morn, when 50% of Aunt Maria was due to be scattered, the Martineau family were at breakfast as usual in the kitchen when Christian asked, "Wasn't it today that you are due to deal with Aunt Mary's ashes?" George leapt up and dashed across to retrieve the sad little brown cardboard box that had been resting forgotten in the vestry. Time was short, so George seized the empty silver cigarette box from the rectory drawing-room on his way back to the kitchen, shaking out tobacco detritus as he ran. He took the spoon out of the marmalade, licked it and spooned half Aunt Mary into the silver box. I understood that he threw the spoon into the washing-up bowl with the dirty breakfast things, but others say that he held it under the tap before plunging it back into the marmalade pot!

And that even is not the end of these unique obsequies. Poor George just made it in time to the top of the hill where the octogenarian Uncle Dick, in a pair of new black boots bought for the occasion, was waiting in the howling east wind and lashing rain with a handful of aged mourners, of whom my parents were the youngest. Hastily shouting a handful of prayers above the turbulent weather, George opened his box and without testing the wind, hurled the 50% of Aunt Maria into the faces of the assembled mourners, who were left spluttering, sneezing and frantically trying to dust her off their wet clothes as best they might. My father concluded his vivid account thus: "She was a damned menace all her life and it was evident that even death itself had failed to effect any improvement".

The third Admiral brother was Stuart, the best looking of the lot and an outstanding golfer, who settled in Sandwich after retiring. My parents often stayed with him and his pleasant, well-endowed wife Daisy, while my father competed at Princes in the annual Parliamentary Golf Handicap. One year he was the winner and chose to buy a vast, mahogany sideboard from Maples with his prize money that stayed with us until my mother's death in 1982. Stuart and Daisy were not as regular visitors to Deeside as some, but we saw a good deal of them and I particularly remember his golf. Sadly he possessed a foul temper, the only bad-tempered Farquhar in the nest, and I believe he earned himself a far from flattering reputation in the Royal Navy. His daughter Mollie married a man named Todd and produced Anne Todd, the actress.

Next, after Stuart, came Mowbray who, being nearer in age to my father and his brothers, was always closer to them and the affairs of their generation and there seems in particular to have been regular and intimate correspondence between him and my father. This possibly came about from Mowbray's military career during both Boer Wars, after which he retired and joined BSA; it was with this company that he designed and produced the Farquhar rifle that I mentioned earlier. Like Stuart, Mowbray and his wife Muriel were in my day only occasional summer visitors to Aboyne and I am left with the impression that he had hung up his guns and fishing rods thereby being somewhat outshone by his brothers on Deeside.

The youngest boy was Bertie, twin brother of Alice the Butterfly, and the ambulance driver in Boulogne (described in chapter two) who looked after my mother (and unconsciously after me too) at the time of my father's wounding. Although not identical, he and Alice were both strikingly good-looking and attractive people and in their later years still full of joie-de-vivre and high spirits. Bertie was the gay, philandering male of the family, just as his sister was the female flirt; albeit he was happily married and deployed his considerable charms with discretion (not so, naughty Alice). His amorous adventures were, perhaps fortunately, restricted by the weakening after-effects of having been gassed in the First World War; and as I've already said, he and his younger brother Hobart, who was killed in that holocaust, were the only two boys of their generation who failed to make 80. My mother had clearly been one of his many conquests and I fancy there had been more than just a whiff of romance between them despite their considerable disparity in age. This conjecture however is based on a schoolboy's sharp, but immature, observations as interpreted many years later.

About him and his twin, Alice, there is a charming tale to tell of their childhood at Drumnagesk. The occasion was another of the large, formal dinner parties thrown by their parents, the old Admiral and Lady Farquhar when the twins were about six years old. All was proceeding smoothly until following the servants in with the entrée came Bertie and Alice, hand-in-hand and stark naked. In dead silence they solemnly paraded once round the dining-room, staring fixedly at the guests, disappearing whence they came through the serving door leaving a stunned Victorian assembly speechless and the servants, laden with dishes, motionless as if struck by sight of Medusa's head. On recovering from shock, their mother hurried after them and discovered that they had covered themselves from head to foot with her vanishing cream, deeming this a foolproof device for discovering unseen what grown-ups got up to after children's bedtime. They must have made a most attractive picture with their early good looks.

I hope these brief sketches of my Farquhar great-aunts and uncles do not give an impression of over-eulogistic admiration or exaggerated eccentricity, for I must firmly assert that I have adhered strictly and accurately to my own recollections and the well-established clan folklore. Any embroidering that my father or anyone else, may have indulged in can safely be discounted as in no way diminishing the underlying truth about them. As you will soon discover, there is more to tell as my recollections unfold.

At the Aboyne Ball. My parents with Aunt Eve and Uncle Arthur and others. I always think that Mother Eve is telling the Admiral to hold his tummy in.
c. 1935

CHAPTER X
Bletsoe

During the inter-war years little changed at Bletsoe and even after the death of Gan-Gan in 1934, Andy kept things much the same. As I have already mentioned, it was a botched amalgamation of a local builder/developer's pair of semis, inoffensive externally, with granite pebble dash locally known as harling and a warren of dark passages within, the walls of which were entirely covered by family photographs of every size, age and consequence. The rooms off these corridors were well-proportioned and there was much good quality Victorian furniture, many more photographs of Gan-Gan's friends and, thank Heaven, comfortable beds upstairs. The only bathroom became, inevitably, the focus of furtive manoeuvring once Gan-Gan's priority session was completed each morning with much scuffling of bedroom slippers up and down the passage. It was a happy house, despite its shortcomings and that, after all, is what really matters – we all enjoyed ourselves.

Like the house, our holiday activities hardly changed over the span of some 15 summers either. Of course, there were for me differences between an eight-year old and a naval officer in his early twenties, just as the acquisition of family cars altered the pattern and scope of our activities somewhat, but all in all, the place, the people and the many pleasures remained happily the same.

Gan-Gan's three servants I mentioned earlier. There was Margaret, the cook who continued in office until only a few years before Andy's death in 1968; a rangy, somewhat forbidding, gypsyish person who cocked her head forwards and to one side, rolling her eyes obliquely upwards when talking to you. She and her kitchen would have caused apoplexy in a health inspector, but she was one of the best game-chefs you could wish for, as well as a good all-round Scottish cook, and we never suffered upset tums.

Next came Barbara, the housemaid, a dark, buxom farmer's daughter with wonderful blue eyes and a ready laugh who was forever teaching us to speak and understand the local Doric — almost a foreign language, so full is it of Scandinavian. And finally Kennedy, who being the parlourmaid, was always addressed by her surname. She was a ginger-headed Scotswoman, distinguished by a surprising pair of gold-rimmed pince-nez on her sharp pointed nose and a propensity for being easily reduced to helpless giggles at the dinner table by the antics, not only of Roger and me, but of my father and Andy also.

A prominent feature of the Bletsoe regime was daily family prayers before breakfast, attended by us boys and the servants, but not our idle parents or Uncle Andy. The three maids were ranged in line in the dining-room before the massive Victorian sideboard facing Gan-Gan who sat at the opposite end of the dining-room table, with Roger and me behind her in the bay window. Close by where we sat stood a bookcase containing a considerable collection of devotional works, doubtless an accumulation from our grandfather's holy office. Here I should explain that Gan-Gan referred to everyone she knew as "Dear So-and-So" while they were alive. After death they became "*Poor* dear So-and-So"; surely an unflattering reflection on their chances in the hereafter, albeit quite unintentional. If the deceased's photograph had been adorning the house, it was now moved to the top of this quasi-sanctified piece of furniture. We discovered that, with a discreet but deliciously risky application of pressure from a furtive foot, it could be made to sway, causing the deceased aloft to rock back and forth, as if bowing gracefully. This danse macabre had the desired effect of reducing the assembled staff to paroxysms of suppressed laughter, spluttering nose-tricks and scarlet faces, and of Gan-Gan, who could not see what was (literally) afoot, pausing in her Bible reading to frown reprovingly over her pince-nez. She must have known we were up to no good, but she never said a word.

Outside the dining-room a small brass gong stood, the sound of which ringing in my memory still evokes thoughts of homemade Scots porridge that had been simmering overnight, herrings split and fried in oatmeal, grouse, Aberdeen-Angus beef, fresh salmon and both strawberries and raspberries, and cream the earlier season of which we had already enjoyed in the South. It was still true in those days that often when engaging servants they stipulated in their terms that they were not to be fed grouse or salmon since they had long since become sick of a surfeit of both. Herrings, black puddings and boiled mutton for them, buried in heaps of mashed tatties and neeps – and for me too, come to that.

The drawing-room at Bletsoe was pleasant, light and airy and large enough to accommodate a family of six and a walnut baby grand comfortably together with Gan-Gan's writing desk and a large bombé fronted Dutch marquetry bureau. Photographs and ornaments abounded everywhere, which led to a regular diversion for the males of the family provided by my mother's perpetual and irreversible addiction to wandering round any room putting things straight – just moving them for moving something's sake. These minor adjustments did not go unnoticed and irritated my otherwise even-tempered grandmother who would exclaim, "Some interfering person has moved this or hidden that" to the world at large, well aware of the culprit's identity; a culprit well practiced in the art of ignoring such sallies. This habit of my mother's had been coarsely, but aptly, dubbed 'fuckering' by my father, who could be equally irritated by her restlessness and from time to time would shout, "Stop fuckering, Madge".

My mother and Gan-Gan were fond enough of one another, but at a distance, as was often then the case between mothers- and daughters-in law of those generations. Each respected the other's qualities and both had senses of humour which prevented the unavoidable strain engendered by, as they say, two vixens down the same hole, breaking cover. Gan-Gan was always 'mother-in-law' to my mother which encapsulates the situation between them in Oxfordshire just as on Deeside. But as I say, they were extremely fond of each other.

Andy had his own sanctum next to the dining-room, redolent of Three Nuns tobacco that he constantly smoked in a meerschaum-shaped pipe, and gun-oil. It was a darkish room, its one window looking out on the verandah, heated by a single-bar electric fire and containing his desk, two well-worn armchairs, a gate-legged table and an oak chest. The built-in bookshelves were stacked with his collection of expensive, erotically illustrated editions of Rabelais, the *1001 Arabian Nights*, the *Decameron* and other similar classics such as *Comus*, as well as a volume entitled *Thaïs* and another I recall entitled *The Garden of Adonis* that certainly would classify today as not-so-soft porn. He also had stacks of bound copies of *La Vie Parisienne*, offset by Punches and Geographical Magazines and on the wall a large reproduction of a Whistler-type lady reclining on a polar bearskin in scanty, see-through, diaphanous wisps, closely resembling the widow whom I have earlier mentioned as the unforthcoming focus of all poor Andy's frustrated romantic attentions. There was a barograph on the chest, which he carefully maintained and which together with the oft-tapped brass ship's barometer on the wall between his study and the dining-room were daily sources of the weather forecasting, freely indulged in by all the clan. All round Aboyne you would hear the Farquhars shouting about it to each other: "Glass falling again, I see, and with this east wind I would expect more rain", or perhaps, "Clouds are down on Cloch-na-Ben (a local hill) and the wind's backing nor-west, so it doesn't look too good for fishing tomorrow" — with that plethora of old salts around, this attention to meteorology could perhaps be expected, since regard for fine weather from the days of sail was part of their living and breathing. This sea-training, combined with local folklore acquired early in life running wild round Drum-nagesk, made them effective and much respected weather prophets. With the enchantment of distance in time, I seem to think they were far better than today's pundits at Bracknell with all their satellites and computers.

This digression on the family's forecasting propensities has led my narrative out of doors and into the village, so I will move on to the bicycle shed, extricate with difficulty my Raleigh bike from the collection of six family and two or three assorted servants' machines and

Gan-Gan's 80th birthday with her four sons

set off to catalogue the salient features of Aboyne itself.

Round the large Green (The Charlestown, you will remember) were inter alia the Wee-Free Kirk whose clock struck the hours but was always wrong, the rather grand Church of Scotland Kirk across from Bletsoe, the Huntly Arms Hotel and the Victory Hall. The last-named is a fine silver-granite memorial building commemorating the two world wars, endowed after the first by Geordie Coats of Coats' Cotton fame who became Lord Glentanar. It contains a beautiful hexagonal sanctuary by the entrance, commemorating the dead and comprises a library, the main hall, containing a fully equipped stage with green rooms behind and a gallery, plus ample service facilities including a caretaker's flat, occupied in those days by another good friend of ours named Bella Crichton. She also presided over the adjoining bowling green and four hard tennis courts; so it was to Bella we first went to acquire our holiday membership of the tennis club. (Also in the main hall you will find honours boards containing the names of all Aboyne's sons and daughters who fought in the two world wars, including my father's, Roger's and mine amongst many uncles and cousins.)

That done, we were off east, through the village to the justly renowned Aboyne golf course to put our clubs in the locker room and join that as well. From the clubhouse, a square pepper-pot bungalow in those days, you looked out on a magnificent view up the valley over the grounds of Aboyne Castle, the seat of Scotland's premier Marquis, Lord Huntly. Alongside the tenth and eleventh holes lay the Aboyne Loch, grave of multitudes of golfballs, in which the nearby purple conical hill of Mortloch with its granite cairn atop was reflected. There would be no time for golf on this first day and I shall come back to what was a salient feature of our Scottish holidays in a later chapter.

Just now, it is on to the bike and back home, obediently getting off at the exceedingly dangerous junction with the main Aberdeen/Braemar road, then down the village brae to the Station Square for a tuppenny slider at the little tobacconist/sweet shop hanging on the parapet above the railway cutting between the station and the long tunnel that gobbled up Aunt Janie. Later, obedience had flown out of the window and I started swerving down onto the A93 without dismounting until, inevitably, I was knocked off and lucky not be be killed one day by, as it turned out, Charles Hambro's yellow Rolls Royce on its way (with my grandmother as a passenger) to Dunecht for Annie Cowdray's annual tea-time rave-up. This was a painful lesson well learnt, but the Hambros gave me a huge box of chocolates to help recovery from my many bruises and soften the impact of the well-earned ticking-off that ensued.

Much later in life it was to George Strachan's royally appointed licenced grocer's shop instead of the tobacconist, for a bottle from his vast collection of single-malt whiskies for which he was and still is revered throughout the north east. He has his photograph framed above the off-licence counter, squatting in the Station Square outside with over 170 different varieties of malt whisky taken by the *Aberdeen Press and Journal* for a feature article.

A few shops away from George there was then Mr Farquharson, the ageing Aberdeen tailor who operated in Aboyne during the season and by whom each year my brother and I were kitted out with a new plus-four suit and matching cap in Harris or Brora tweed. These were fitted in time to be christened at the Aboyne Games on the first September Saturday.

Also on that side of the square, John Troup, for many years the Farquhar family butcher, had his shop and I am pleased to say his successors are still in business there selling the best Aberdeen-Angus beef that I have ever known, of which they send us a sirloin every month by parcel post. It gets well hung on its journey and in well over 30 years, we have only had to bury two.

The Dee Valley is wide here and Aboyne sits raised a little above the river on its north bank, in a beautiful amphitheatre formed by the heather and pine-clad foothills of the Cairngorms. The blue-painted suspension bridge emblazoned with the Huntly coat of arms has long since been replaced by a wider, single-span bridge of granite and reinforced concrete that fits amiably enough into its surroundings. It has ever been a local habit in idle moments to take a dander down to the bridge and count the salmon lying below and the more so now that polaroid spectacles make spotting the king of fish so much easier.

One other important feature of Aboyne life that deserves mention here is the Scottish Episcopal Church of St Thomas's, built of silver granite on a beautiful wooded site beside the Ballater road. It is a copy of an Italian renaissance church and was given to the diocese by Lord Glentanar, who you will recall also built and endowed the Victory Hall. It is a pleasant and resonant building and the scene of regular church parades attended by all the piscies for miles around. Great was the chat outside after matins. Here it was that Great-Uncles Arthur, Dick and Charlie and later Uncle Andy, read the lessons so well. My father teased Uncle Arthur once after taking a particularly long second lesson from Corinthians by remarking to him that it was a pity the postcard was not invented in St Paul's day.

It is of course to be expected, following another world war, that changes should occur over the 40 or 50 years that have elapsed since the time that I am writing about – especially following the development of the North Sea oilfields – and changes there certainly have been at Aboyne. These, however, are mostly on the outskirts of the village. The Green, the Station Square, the Victory Hall, the Huntly Arms Hotel, the two kirks, the cattle market and most of the surrounding buildings in the heart of Aboyne remain much as they were. Alas, most of the people are gone and that is why I felt I should try, in my untutored way, to describe them and their activities and not only just in Aboyne itself, but throughout the county, for they were indeed a diverse and colourful lot.

CHAPTER XI

Golf

Golf at Aboyne deserves a chapter to itself for it played so large a part in ours, and everyone else's lives. All the clan, from eight to 80 played, none badly, most to good average 12 to 18 handicap and two or three in single figures.

Being Scotland, all the locals played too and very well as a rule (as for instance Walter Wright, the Aboyne electrician, who won the Worplesdon mixed foursomes with his wife) plus many of the regular summer visitors. A morning round of 18 or 11 holes was virtually a daily routine. Of the 18-hole course, the first ten and the seventeenth and eighteenth are on low undulating grassland, and from the eleventh to the sixteenth up and down the considerable humps and hollows at the foot of Mortloch. The latter have always been known as The Hilly Holes and lazy or elderly golfers often skipped them by playing on to the sixteenth green from the eleventh tee – an easy number nine iron. There have been many hot disputes over such cutting in over the years.

In our day the course was grazed by black-faced sheep, whose droppings were a natural hazard but when dried out enough came in handy for practice swings; the groundsmen were forever clearing them off the unguarded greens, but you took your chance on the fairways and in the rough. Their perpetrators, on fine days, were often to be found sunbathing in the bunkers and they were frequently hit by golf-balls, to which through their wool they were impervious.

In high season, the roaring of the Farquhars echoed round the adjoining Loch, greeting each other, swopping scores or in angry dispute over the finer interpretations of the R&A rules. Uncle Arthur was perhaps the canniest and most effective, though not the best performer. Apart from knowing every blade of grass on the course better than most, he had a sure-fire match winning device in the form of an oval aluminium ball-cleaner containing a sponge that, having never seen water, had atrophied into the consistency of a pebble. This he produced on the green while his opponent was lining up his putt, as if making ready to clean his ball as soon as play at that hole was over. Au moment critique, as the enemy's putter was pulled back for the strike, he would give his ball-cleaner a sharp rattle that never failed to achieve the desired result. What made it all impossibly difficult for his victims was their sure knowledge of what was about to occur.

Andy, as earlier mentioned, was a real freak at golf. Having absolutely no match temperament he got into a fearful stew almost before he started to play. He was basically a thumper, raising his club high above his head with arms extended backwards from which unpromising posture, and after a short tensed pause, he brought it down with a grunt and an earth-shattering crash, knees bent forward and chin tightly tucked into his chest. His younger brother, Dick, unkindly claimed that Andy did better playing east to west as his technique was designed to stop the world going round while his ball went on.

Uncle Dick St John was himself quite a spectacle playing golf; feet spread wide apart, always with a long cigarette holder stuck out of the left corner of his mouth, breathing stentoriously through his badly broken nose while he waggled the club for ages before as it were catching his ball unawares.

Here I digress for a moment to tell you something of Dick, the youngest of the four St John brothers, which is not inappropriate since to think of him is to think of golf. After being axed like Andy from the navy as a Commander in 1923 he joined BSA and later became Managing Director of their then subsidiary Daimler Hire where he reigned with much success over their garages in Knightsbridge, living with his second wife Peggy in Montpelier Square. Physically he was principally distinguished by this pugilist's nose sustained in childhood when his brothers, who had been compelled to walk, ambushed him biking home to Drumnagesk from church at Kincardine-O'Neil and pushed a stick into his front wheel. Of rugged build and great good humour, he was a born clubman and bon viveur, spending much of his considerable leisure time playing golf. He was Captain of Wentworth for several years after he and Peggy had moved to a house on that estate in the later '30s and was also a member of Sunningdale and Swinley Forest.

One day when he was playing with Stuart Farquhar at St George's he was waggling away at his ball on the twelfth tee as a group of workmen were cycling by on their way back to Princes' after the lunch-break. They went slower and slower waiting to see Dick's drive till, losing patience and wobbling madly, one of them shouted over his shoulder "Hit it you ____!", whereupon Dick buried his ball in deep rough 12 feet ahead of the tee and Stuart remarked laconically "Damn good eyesight that chap has".

On another occasion, while playing at Swinley Forest, he found a couple engaged in country matters in the bunker where he had put his ball; nothing loth he blasted it out covering the gentleman's bare posterior aspect in sand who only then acknowledged the presence of others in his cosy corner. Looking up at Dick he remarked with some heat, "Ain't you got no bloody shame?" But back to Aboyne golf course.

Andy enhanced his entertainment value enormously by his propensity for finding an excuse for his many wild shots; playing very short at the par three ninth, for instance, he once exclaimed, "Did you see that? My ball definitely fell into an air pocket". Of course someone had to say that he was once put off by the roaring of the butterflies in the neighbouring meadows – I think it was my father.

The world was far safer for children in those days and on the rare occasions that I found myself without a partner, I would think nothing of teaming up with total strangers. I once did this with a man who it transpired came from South Africa. It was soon clear to me that not only was he a lousy golfer, but that he also must have been rich for he proceeded to fire a succession of brand new Dunlop balls all over the place and not once did we bother to look for them. Naturally, I had carefully marked them and returned that afternoon to reap a rich harvest.

A person to avoid on the golf course, if possible, was Angie Swain, the Bishop of Lincoln's wife, who was surely the slowest player ever and nursed an unshakable conviction that her place on the course was sacrosanct. Her technique involved attempting to mesmerise the ball by staring motionless at it for several minutes before starting a slow series of spasmodic movements, rather like a mechanical figure striking an aged town clock; often the long-delayed result would be a clean miss and the tedious process restarted. At best she would propel it for not more than 50 yards and the mesmerisms started all over again. The Bish wisely never played with her, usually teaming up with Uncle Charlie arrayed always in brightly contrasted black and white, pepper and salt baggy tweeds.

Once each holiday, the Tudor St Johns played a family foursome; elder brother Roger and Mama, a poor performer who really disliked the game, and me with Papa. Why we persisted with this event remains a mystery, for without fail it ended in a blazing row of splendid proportions, floods of tears from Mother and sons and a purple, apoplectic Pater Familias. Such however was its ferocity that the storm soon blew itself out leaving harmony and laughter safely restored.

The Deeside railway ran past the Loch and close alongside the long eighth hole where I have many times had to cross the line to look for my sliced drive. This hole provided a perfect vantage point from which to wave at close range to the King and Queen on their way at a stately pace behind a pilot engine in the magnificent Royal Train that was then chocolate and cream and very long. King George V and Queen Mary, and later George VI and Queen Elizabeth, always spent the entire journey from Aberdeen to Ballater waving at the people lining the route from their drawing-room car. It was an immense thrill for a schoolboy such as I to be so close and feel such an intimate contact with these legendary persons.

I am glad to say this cosy local Scottish course in its outstanding setting is little changed and I could take you there and show you the more fruitful areas of search for pick-ups and recall a thousand incidents as we walked round, like on the third when, aged about ten, I hit a miraculous shot and stunned an aged lady putting ahead. The only changes are definitely for the better – no more black-faced sheep for instance, and the pepper-pot bungalow of yore replaced by a splendid two-storey clubhouse, fully licenced and with a dining-room, lounge and generous picture windows from which to enjoy that unique Deeside vista up to Loch-na-gar.

The Loch has become a pleasure centre with a holiday camp on its island and is none the worse for that, though you might perhaps be put off hitting your second at the tenth hole by the shouts and screams of water-skiers. Until this innovation, its sole recreational contribution, apart from its beauty, had been a Bon Spiel (that is a curling tourney) when it froze hard enough, for which the Deeside railway once installed a special halt – already redundant in our day.

The 11th Marquess of Huntley in his youth

Craigveigh, Aboyne. The two yew trees were christened Madge and Tudor

CHAPTER XII

The denizens of Aboyne

Having digressed about the four Aboyne Farquhars and some of the village tradesmen, I now turn to some of the other notables living there in the '20s and '30s, the most distinguished of whom must I suppose be the old Marquis of Huntly. He was head of the Clan Gordon, 'Cock of the North', Premier Marquis of Scotland with a quiverful of other titles and by my time already flat broke, having successfully gambled away his entire fortune and estates within a few years of coming into his inheritance as a young man. Then in his eighties he was still a striking figure, slim, erect and topping six feet with the renowned good looks of the Gay Gordons (a sobriquet doubtless less popular now in these so-called enlightened days, but still flattering then), set off by silken silvery locks and sweeping moustache. In full highland kit, with the three eagle's feathers of a paramount chieftain waving a foot or more above his bonnet, he was a magnificent sight presiding over the Aboyne Games. He is reported as saying while out shooting on Peter Hill, which commands a vista of lower Deeside and the coast of Angus for fully 20 miles in all directions, "All you can see from here was mine when I came into the title. Now all that is left is the Feu on the Charlestown of Aboyne" ie the manorial rights on the village green. He had saved himself from Carey Street by marrying late in life a fat, unattractive and common but immensely rich American lady from Chicago with an equally unattractive grown-up son named Arthur

Campbell who assumed the title "Hon" when his mother made herself a Marchioness.

Huntly was her third husband and she was fond of proclaiming, and on one occasion in my hearing, "The first time I married, I married for love. The second time for money and the third time I married Huntly for his title. But my son, Arthur, he's the child of love". Huntly himself had never been inattentive to affairs of the heart and clearly many maidens had fallen for his remarkable charms as witness the occasional handsome Grieve or Ghillie around the district who might have been mistaken for the old boy.

He, the Marchioness and the awful Arthur occupied a suite of rooms at the Huntly Arms where, they say, Arthur was once discovered asleep on the floor outside his mother's bedroom door, "Preventing my stepfather pinching Mother's jewels". Huntly had the charming, courtly manners of the Grand Seigneur to match his good looks and was, in consequence, loved by all and forgiven the many manifest wickednesses which he for all his time most grievously had committed.

For some unaccountable reason, the four of us were invited every year to supper at the hotel with the Huntlys, playing rummy afterwards in their private sitting-room. The food was cold and indifferent and we played for matchsticks, but the old boy greatly enjoyed himself; I think he missed having children – that is to say children that he could acknowledge. Later they adopted twin girls from America, who were also dubbed as "Hons" and tricked out inappropriately in highland regalia.

Aboyne Castle, the Huntly seat, was by the '30s a dangerous ruin and the estate in hock to a local entrepreneur named Raggy Mearns. Later, when old Huntly died, his great-nephew, Charles Gordon, inherited and he having married Lord Kemsley's daughter, Pamela Berry, was able to buy back the estate and start the long process of rehabilitation, eventually turning it over to his son and heir, Granville Aboyne. He in turn completed the process, having married an heiress, Jane Gibbs, one of Lord Cowdray's nieces. Granville and Jane knocked down the ugly and rotted Victorian additions and completely refurbished the original keep with great skill and good taste.

I progress naturally from the Marquis of Huntly to his kindly, but very pompous cousin Gordon Duncan who had grown up with my father on Deeside, with his somewhat older, regal lady-wife, Isobel, sometime lady-in-waiting to HRH Princess Marie-Louise ("My Princess"), whose silver-framed photograph occupied pride of place on the grand piano. Gordon was a highly skilled and successful geologist and consultant mining engineer, responsible inter alia for the discovery of rich veins of copper in Cyprus. He was a stout, sallow man, bald and with a vast walrus moustache that he kept on biting when he spoke causing him to emit strange mumblings and grunts. He was a pillar of the piscy church and in later years, clad of course in his kilt took his turn reading the second Lesson. When Andrew was three years old or so, Pam and I took him to matins at St Thomas's and afterwards my father asked him what he had seen. "I saw God in a red skirt" was the reply, which explains perhaps my son's readiness later to embrace J P Sartre's existentialist philosophies with such eagerness.

Isobel had the most bulging eyes and prominent bosom that I have ever seen, the former behind thick pebble glasses and the latter heroically corsetted and frigidly décolleté. She and Gordon were incurable but kindly snobs even changing the name of their house from Ladywood Lodge to *The* Ladywood Lodge when they bought it. Gordon considered himself an Extremely Important Person and I have to say that probably to an extent he was, for it is true that whenever he travelled south or arrived from London by train, the stationmaster at Aberdeen would meet him in top hat and morning-dress, an honour vouchsafed to Royalty and the highest in the land, and he could always get you a sleeper in the difficult war years when they were like gold. When war was declared, Gordon had telegraph poles erected all over the Aboyne green to prevent German aircraft landing to capture him. Having grown up with my father and uncles he was a close and valued friend. Indeed, the Duncans were friends with everyone and their innocent foibles caused only friendly amusement and mild leg-pulling since, like so many of the people I am remembering, Gordon and Isobel were among the kindest and most generous of couples.

A post-war example of Gordon's good-natured self-importance concerns the Humber Snipe his firm gave him on his retirement, which he nursed with great care for quite a few more years until he became too old to drive. By then he knew of our connection with Geoffrey Rootes which he invoked by writing to ask for an appointment on urgent matters at Devonshire House. We later learnt of this from Geoffrey who was amazed to find himself lunching portentously with this strange old boy solely for the purpose of getting him, Lord Rootes as chairman of the group, to dispose of this ancient relic to a good home and at a good price. This Geoffrey, always generous to a fault, subsequently pretended he had done and Gordon was happily unaware of the sacrifice involved or the car's disposal on the scrapheap.

Towards the end of the war the Duncans, with us and several others, were having drinks with our family doctor Bill Brodie-Brown and his wife Babs the back of whose property overlooked the Deeside railway up which the King and Queen were due to pass. The Brodie-Browns possessed a vast, asthmatic bulldog – also known as Bill – of amiable inquisitiveness and goodly age. He was roaming round the lawn snuffling, head down after crumbs (we were drinking outside on a fine evening) when he chanced to find his way between the stout straddled legs of the kilted Gordon, waffling away with a large whisky in his hand. Puzzled by this sudden eclipse of the sun, Bill the bulldog thrust his mighty, ice-cold slavering muzzle upwards with instant, spectacular results – words are inadequate to describe poor Gordon's discomfort or our hysterical hilarity; suffice it to say the Royal Train passed unnoticed.

Nearby The Ladywood Lodge lived the Dugdale family in their large riverside Victorian villa, Gordon Lodge. They, like Gordon Duncan, had grown up with my father and uncles and were still very much in evidence. Old Ma Dugdale was seeing out her last days tended by her one son, Alfred, and four varied and talented daughters, all of whom she did her best to make ridiculous by her flights of eulogistic romanticising, one early quotation from which (Andy is my source) will serve to define: "Una is my songbird, Daisy my flower, Joan my helpmeet and Rosalind my butterfly, but *Alfred* (pronounced Awlfred) is my standard-bearer". As the standard-bearer in question was the only one without much intelligence, physically a weed and cursed with a repellant wall eye, this claim led only to merciless ridicule. Una became a leading suffragette with the Pankhursts, persuading Joan to join her; both went to prison and it was Una, I think, who went on hunger-strike and suffered the inhuman torture of force-feeding. She eventually married a man named Duval (details unknown) and Joan an Indian army colonel called Cruikshank. It was upon Daisy and her consular officer husband Alured Cunninghame, who had lost his left leg in the First World War, that the burden mostly fell of looking after the old lady and Gordon Lodge, so we saw quite a lot of them and very charming they were.

But the youngest, Rosalind, was you might say, the eighth wonder of the world and very much part of our Aboyne summers. Gregarious beyond belief, unstoppable in her multifarious social activities and enthusiasms right on into her eighties. She had married a rich Yorkshireman named Harrison-Broadley and produced one son and two daughters, June and Heather, who were our regular companions. She had long since left him with what must have been a more than handsome settlement, for she lived the life of O'Reilly and was bedizened with diamonds, including so many heavy bracelets that you wondered how she raised her arm. She was no beauty, having a prominent nose, horse-like teeth and a receding chin, but those blemishes were amply offset by large cornflower-blue eyes, fluttering eyelashes, peerless complexion and her engaging air of breathless expectancy and excitement. She must have been attractive for my Uncle Dick St John, among others, still carried a flickering torch for her even in our day much to his wife Aunt Peggy's wrath, who used to mock him by neighing and saying, "Dick's off to the stables again" when he went to visit Rosalind. Andy on these occasions was wont typically to quote Shakespeare "As the hart will to the hind, so will I to Rosalind".

Balls, picnics and parties and the secret of eternal youth were Rosalind's perpetual pursuits, plus a strong appetite for 'tuft-hunting' for she was yet another harmless snob. She docked tens of years off her age and made all her grandchildren call her Aunt. One of them, June's daughter Davina Galitza of skiing fame, at one time had a walkout with Jamie Fife (The Duke of That Ilk and related to Royalty to boot) and Rosalind, in seventh Heaven, gushed it all out to my mother . . . "Madge, my dear, Davina is going out with Jamie *Fife!*" — much emphasis on Fife. But my mother wasn't really listening and said, "Oh really? Anything to do with bananas?" Not popular.

As children the Dugdales were closely involved with the four St John brothers, legions of Farquhar cousins and indeed, many of the neighbouring lairds. It is related that while playing mixed cricket on the green, one of the St Johns struck a female Dugdale with a fierce haymaking drive and was immediately challenged to a duel by the infant standard-bearer. It is also hinted strongly that as they grew older picnics up the Fungle, a local secluded beauty spot, supplanted cricket and provided an idyllic setting for exploring la différence – (one of Andy's sly innuendoes). They all attended a Miss Ledingham's kindergarten and when this lady had lived to be 100, her former pupils then in their seventies, threw a tea party for her with a cake and all. Gordon Duncan and Rosalind Harrison-Broadley were both present and it was, of course, Andy who noted that Gordon, who loyally added ten years to his age to match the older Isobel, and Rosalind, who as I've remarked took at least ten years off hers, thus had a declared age difference of over 20 years and yet still managed to share an infants' class with Miss Ledingham. As they were amongst old friends this sally caused no offence but much merriment.

As we and her daughters grew older, Rosalind's schemes for our enjoyment grew from tennis-parties, picnics and dangerous swimming in the Dee above the Aboyne Bridge into more sophisticated ploys. She became a leading hostess and energetic organiser of the 'Pauper's Picnic' dances that had become such a feature of the Deeside season. These were given in turn by a succession of hostesses providing the venue and the band (always Annie Shand's – an expert on Highland dancing) while the others made up parties bringing contributions of food and drink. They were frequent and hugely popular with all ages. Programmes were still de rigueur then and every fourth dance was either a reel or a Scottish country dance which everyone knew and at which most were highly proficient, the majority of males being kilted.

On one occasion when Roger was about 18 and I 14, she overreached herself by throwing a fancy dress evening garden party at Gordon Lodge for all the county jeunesse for which instead of relying on

In the rain at the Aboyne Games. From left to right: Lord Huntly, Frank
Davison, the Neville Chamberlains, Uncle Arthur but not Aunt Eve!

the well-tried and excellent local caterers, she grandly booked a well-known London firm at what must have been considerable expense. They produced cocktails to get the party going, of which being too young at the time I luckily did not partake. Those who did were instantly struck down with violent poisoning. I remember having to support my legless, six foot four inch, hefty brother home to nearby Bletsoe on foot. The party was over in less than half an hour; but I don't think poor Rosalind had the nerve to sue the said firm whose staff must surely have used wood alcohol in the drinks.

As time went on, Rosalind's sway over the Deeside social scene became virtually absolute and by the time I had children old enough to do a season up there she was still in the lead and no-one dared go to a ball before attending one of "Mrs Harrison-Broadley's highland dance coaching sessions".

Aboyne in those days contained a trio of remarkable widows who were old family friends of ours, and since her grandly-named semi Granville Lodge was close by the Dugdales, I will first dwell for a while on Gan-Gan's close confidante Hilda FitzClarence, whose Naval Captain swain had long since departed and been buried beside the path at St Thomas's. She was Aunt Hilda to most of the locality, much like my grandmother, but there the resemblance ended for she was very thin, anaemic and devoid of any colour, with bloodless lips and the palest of grey eyes. She took herself very seriously and cultivated a somewhat grand and well-informed manner in the nicest and quite harmless way. Hence the house's pretentious name and her style of living which was precious and studied. She always wore black, grey or white; usually expensive silk blouses from Debenhams with well-tailored suits and a succession of expensive hats with veils and black satin bows. She kept two full-time domestics and a daily, plus a chauffeur for her adored Humber touring car and a jobbing gardener, Geordie Milne, whom she shared with my grandmother – altogether quite an establishment even in those days for an elderly widow with a bird-like appetite living for most of the year alone.

Aunt Hilda spent much time motoring about the county, visiting, sight-seeing and above all, scouring the many and alas sometimes not too honest antique dealers abounding on Dee and Donside. She was a compulsive spender and an avid collector of bibelots of all sorts, which she lavished on herself and all her friends. These generous gifts included many to the St John family, some of which adorn our house to this day — the cordial bottles on our drawing-room window-sill for instance.

She talked incessantly through her nose in a creamy, high-pitched monotone mostly about her servants and her possessions, extant or newly-acquired, and many of these digressions concerned adventures with the motor-car and its faithful guardian, the chauffeur Femister. There had been trouble on the way to Aberdeen, she would report, resulting in Femister with his head buried under the bonnet and Aunt Hilda sitting regally rugged on the back seat. "After a while I said to Femister 'I think it must be something to do with the carburettor' and when he had examined it he replied 'Mrs Fitzclarence, Madam, you are quite right'". Of course, she had little or no idea what a carburettor was or what it looked like but Femister, who had just cleaned the distributor head, knew his onions alright; he would have done well in the Foreign Office.

It was Aunt Hilda's unshakable routine to spend a fortnight each summer at the club in Edinburgh for a change of air and shops and to allow the servants a short break (but only after they had thoroughly spring-cleaned the house). One year the aforementioned jobbing gardener, Geordie Milne, had fallen seriously ill a week or so before her departure and was not expected to last long. But the date of departure arrived and Geordie was still with us so, not wishing to miss out on the anticipated obsequies, she procured a vast wreath, full of heather and spagnum moss and called upon a willing Aunt Addie to give it house-room and in due course to hand it in for Geordie's funeral. Geordie, however was a bibulous old rogue and like many locals must have got at the whisky bottle after she had left, which effectively repelled the Great Reaper. Thus the St Johns were left suffering great bathtime discomfort at Bletsoe for over a week, occasioned by the sharp, gritty and intrusive bits shed by that damned wreath while it was being kept fresh in the only bath, and which invaded every crevice of the human frame. At last, Gan-Gan was compelled to oust the nuisance in the face of a

The Aboyne Ball again. Back row: Gordon and Isobel Gordon-Duncan my
Father and A.N. Other. Front row: my Mother, Charlie Huntly and Lily
Singer

united crescendo of complaints from her entire household and was seen disappearing with it over the handlebars of her bike. We were curious to learn what she had done with it and all was revealed next Sunday when, on our way up the path to Church, we spotted the wreath adorning the late Captain FitzClarence's grave. My grandmother had omitted to read the attached black-edged visiting-card in the haste engendered by her Scots instinct of avoiding waste. Not so my father who, to everyone's utter delight, discovered that under her name Hilda had written, "In token of many years' faithful service". Gan-Gan cried laughing all through matins, but I don't think Hilda was ever told.

To find the next widow, we go over to the south side of the river, up a well kept by-road leading to Balfour, home of the Cochrane family, passing Birse Loch, a justly renowned, quiet beauty spot where old Lady Glentanar had built a heather-thatched summer-house for Queen Mary, who loved to come there to picnic alone with the King.

Further on, in a handsome granite house lived Lily Singer, but before I tell of her I will take you past her house to a disused granite quarry deeply filled with clear water where we and our friends were wont to go swimming in the hot weather. It happened one day that I was rushing back on my bike, full tilt down the hill, bathers and towel streaming in the wind and late as usual for a punctual Bletsoe lunch after a morning swim, when round a bend I found myself confronted by the oncoming Royal Daimler filling the road between the park-palings as snugly as a piston in a cylinder. Skidding madly, I ended up in a deep, narrow ditch pressed frantically against the palings, bike buried beneath me, staring straight up at Queen Mary, the Daimler having come to a sudden and unceremonious halt alongside me. She and the King always sat on the folding seats of their limousine when they went touring, the better to admire the scenery. So there she was winding down the window with King George V peering anxiously over her shoulder at yours truly, cap in hand, dishevelled and doubtless scarlet with embarrassment.

All was well, however, as they were both most kind and smiling and – in retrospect – I don't doubt relieved to find me breathing. The Queen asked if I were hurt, and they were relieved to learn that no damage had been done. Anyway I got no ticking-off for being dangerously out of control. The chauffeur looked pretty sour though.

But about Lily Singer. Her maiden name was Grahame and she treasured her Scottish connections. She had been married to Paris Singer, whom she divorced in a famous, much publicised affair after he had gone off to live unmarried with the celebrated Isadora Duncan, founder, it is generally accepted, of modern dance. Paris's life must have been tragic. A fantastically rich co-heir of the Singer Sewing Machine fortune, he was lucky to escape as a regular submariner from his 'K' boat in the infamous 'Battle of Bass Rock', one of the worst disasters ever. Then, having wrecked his marriage with Lily and never seeing their only daughter Winaretta again, his and Isadora's children were drowned in the Seine when the brakes of the car in which they had been taken out failed and it rolled backwards off the quay. Finally of course, Isadora was killed in front of him when her scarf caught in the chain-drive of the Bugatti in which she was being driven off after a riotous party by one of the Jeunesse Doré. He and Lily had once lived in the vast Palladian Singer Mansion in Paignton and after it had been presented to the municipality, she bought a small villa nearby on the sea-front where she wintered and in which she often entertained me and other naval cadets from Dartmouth to sumptuous Sunday blow-outs that included pounds of Devonshire cream.

She also had a pied-à-terre in London, but being a Scot it was in her Aboyne house, Praesmohr, that she spent most of her life and in which during the Second World War she eventually died, leaving some fine furniture and pictures to my parents, of whom she was extremely fond. They added considerably to this bequest at the subsequent house-sale which, thanks to the war, produced an abundance of excellent bargains. I believe Lily would have been pleased with this.

She was gregarious and generous and had long been accustomed to hosting large, varied and, I dare say, often Bohemian house-parties. She still entertained lavishly if more quietly, but had retained her outré, and somewhat eccentric, taste with lots of costly lacquer chinoiserie, Lalique glass and art nouveau enamel scattered amongst her antique furniture. She was usually to be found playing bridge or mah-jongg for high stakes, chain-smoking Turkish or Russian cigarettes through a long ivory holder clenched in her teeth between the thin lips she had slashed vividly with lipstick, her white hair cut short and brushed back under a tortoiseshell Alice band. When alone, she worked incessantly and expertly on her needlework, producing many fine silk tapestry pictures and covering chairs and stools galore, including the stool that now stands before the fire in our drawing-room.

She lavished affection on her aged, ill-tempered peke named Ho-ti whose teeth had luckily long since fallen out. It was always wheezing asthmatically on her lap and at meals would be invited to lick the double cream off a silver spoon. Ho-ti had the most penetrating halitosis and a propensity for letting off carpet-creepers far in excess of any other animal I have encountered. Early in life I concluded that Lily, being perpetually lost in clouds of rich cigarette smoke, never noticed those deadly Peking odours.

Lady King is the third widow I wish to tell of, who at first lived when in Scotland at Craigveigh, the house immediately behind and above Bletsoe that eventually became my parents' home for the last 40 years of their lives. Geraldine King was a sister of Alfred and Vere Harmsworth, later to become Lords Northcliffe and Rothermere. Her husband, Sir Lucas King, who died in the middle '20s, had been a distinguished member of the Indian Civil Service, and her only surviving son, Cecil, became chairman and proprietor of IPC and the Mirror Group. We also saw something of her in the south where she lived at Runnymede and Cecil was a perpetual visitor to the Old Mill House in the '20s when he was up at Christchurch. He became closely attached to my parents during that time and, until he finally retired to Dublin in a huff having been ousted from IPC by his own protégé Hugh Cudlipp, always kept in close touch with them. He lived for some time at Culham Court near Henley while we were at Southwood and he also owned a small estate in Aberdeenshire called Cushnie, so either way we were neighbours of the King family.

Lady King sold Craigveigh in the '30s and moved to a large house that she had improved to the west of the village which she named Roebuck. It stands in its own attractive grounds on a highish bank above the river and commands a fine view up the Glen to Ballater and beyond. (It was this house that Pam's Great-Aunt Helen McConnell bought in the early '40s and renamed Lys-na-Greyne.)

Geraldine King was very much *the* Harmsworth, with a large, rugged and commanding presence and a formidable intellect that I suspect outpaced both her distinguished brothers. Physically I could describe her as a better looking, female version of Winston Churchill and her manner could be aptly described as Churchillian. Very much the matriarch (she had three daughters as well as Cecil); one loved and feared her simultaneously. This arose, I think, because of her penetrating perception of people and events that brooked no argument or prevarication and her outspoken directness that bared the truth but was never unkind. She was deeply interested in people as individuals and their problems, towards which she brought wisdom, a generous mind and a strong underlying affection.

One of her daughters, Enid, married an Irishman called Stokes, who became a fanatical Roman Catholic convert. In due course, their equally fanatical son taught History to Andrew at Winchester when the period under review was the Reformation and so nearly succeeded in proselytising him that I made tentative plans for Andrew to see Bishop Wilson of Chichester, a Wykhamist like Andrew from Toyes. This was shortly before J P Sartre and existentialism came to hold the stage so I need not have worried.

Lady King had adopted her orphaned grandson, John Falls, who was the delight of her life and whom she thoroughly spoiled. He was a bit younger than me, played no games and while still under the aegis of a nanny had a slide in his hair that finally condemned him to the rubbish-heap in my schoolboy opinion. He was the epitome of the only child. The Falls saga was tragically repetitive for in due time John and his wife were killed in a flying accident in Egypt, leaving two children whom Cecil King in his turn adopted and brought up with his own family.

Lady King possessed a stately black Rolls Royce limousine of which she was very proud. So proud, it transpired, that when she died they found she had deposed that she was to be borne in it to her funeral at St Thomas's. This wish was duly honoured by hacking out the back of the car. I am told her cortège was a very remarkable sight and the Rolls' bodywork wrecked for life.

Other denizens there were, of course, including two families of Davidsons of Altdinnie (next to the Charlie Farquhars) and of Minarloch (up the Ballater road) that had been Gan-Gan's first Bletsoe. More widows, of whom 'Wagga' Williams was one whose very pleasant Australian granddaughter named Ethel Raffan was one of the gang with us. (The old girl's nickname arose from some nervous affliction that caused her to keep shaking her head.) There was Geordie Coats's widow at Craig-an-Dinnie, old Lady Glentanar (a Wellesley) who, like Lady King, sailed around in a black chauffeur-driven Rolls. She looked to me like a highly-painted Pekinese.

But I think, to quote Private Eye, "Thats'h enough denizensh" and you may, I fear, be bored if I fail to change the subject and start a new chapter.

Pic-nic on the Spittal of Glenshee: from left to right, Desmond FitzGerald, Tudor St John, Ernie and Katie Broadhurst and Madge St John

CHAPTER XIII

Lairs and visitors

In order to enlarge on the Deeside Autumn season and its glories during the inter-war years I must describe the more notable and to us best known inhabitants of Aberdeenshire and its regular summer visitors who helped to make it all possible.

Most of the estates were still occupied by the families who had owned them for many generations and the big houses, many of them castles, full of shooting parties. In addition, from July to October, came a regular clientèle of summer visitors renting villas or hunting lodges up and down Dee and Donside, many like the Farquhars with strong local connections. A host of people of all ages, from four to God knows what, and all bent on taking full advantage of everything the Highlands had to offer. It was the Glorious Twelfth and the grouse-shooting that took pride of place, often enhanced for house-parties by evenings fishing dry-fly for sea-trout on the Don or trying the Autumn salmon run that then still prevailed on the Dee. Grouse and fish were plentiful in those comparatively unpolluted and better controlled days.

Then there were the big social occasions like the Northern Meeting in Inverness, the Aboyne Ball of which my father was for many years the secretary, the Perth Hunt Ball, the Braemar and Aboyne Games and all with what I might term a running base accompaniment of picnic dances, theatre shows in Aberdeen, tennis tournaments, golf, elaborate expeditions to beauty spots and so forth.

Prominent in my life among the visitors to Aboyne itself were the two daughters of the old Admiral Fane who had lived on Deeside: Evelyn, known always as 'E' and married to Jack Taylor the Riviera estate agent and British Vice-Consul at Cannes; and Christina, widow of Count von Metternich whom she had married in 1913 only to find him interned in 1916 at Donnington Hall for the rest of the war where he contracted the TB which killed him shortly after his release. E and Jack's only child was the attractive, gamine Jacqueline with whom I was later secretly in love. Christina had a son Peter, the same age as myself and my constant companion on the golf-course as elsewhere, and a daughter Monica. The two families shared the same house, helped by Jacqueline's M'lle and Jack's Basque chauffeur/handyman and as they were all bilingual or better it was like the upper room at Pentecost.

Although E was almost stone deaf she was an excellent pianist, who loved to play both jazz and classics. We raved about the former, and Roger went everywhere with his drums so we had lots of jam sessions chez Taylor. Jack, who was a great player with the girls, possessed a vast Itala sports tourer in which he once drove my mother backwards to Bletsoe through Aboyne from the Huntly Arms (where they had been enjoying a morning snort) with her screaming with fright all the way. He also took a large party of us at speed up to Ballater to see the King and Queen arrive and inspect the Guard of Honour before they motored on to Balmoral. The car was so crammed that the tiny chauffeur in his Basque beret lay full length between the bonnet and the offside mudguard holding on to the bar that carried the huge headlights – a regular practice it seems whenever the car was full. His beret remained firmly fixed at its usual angle at all speeds.

My mucker Peter, being a Roman Catholic, was at Downside but when he was 16 Christina took him and Monica back to the Metternich estates in Germany, as Peter was by then a Prince as titular head of the family. Sadly they never returned; we heard that both Peter and Monica had been swept up by the euphoria of the Hitler Jugend. I was told he was later killed on the Russian front, but I never knew what happened to Monica. It still gives me cause for thought that two such close and altogether amiable friends should have been engulfed by the evil passions of the Third Reich. It poses the daunting question — what would we in the UK have done under similar circumstances?

Jacqueline subsequently married a man named Montague and now runs the Jack Taylor Estate Agency from Cannes which she helped to revive after its eclipse during the occupation. Jack and E had only narrowly escaped Vichy by car to the Spanish border after he had with great difficulty managed to evacuate the remaining British residents to Barcelona on a coal-ship. They included Somerset Maugham, who was far from helpful, delaying the ship's urgent departure by turning up late and defying the Vice-Consul's instructions to bring one suitcase only. He arrived alongside the ship with copious bags and a huge wooden chest stuffed with costly comestibles which he and his manservant refused to share with their starving fellow passengers.

Moving westward up the Dee you come to Dinnet, the large and attractive estate that Malcolm Barclay-Harvey, the local Tory MP with his effusive and pretty wife Joan and only child Violet had inherited from Sir Henry Brooke. Malcolm was a friend of the family's since his and my father's childhood days, another honorary uncle and frequently host to us four St Johns at Dinnet, a king-sized Edwardian granite pile standing high on a heather-clad escarpment bordering the Dee. The estate included the nearly 2,900 foot renowned local landmark Morven and its attendant shoulder Culblean, scene of a battle in which the locals trapped part of General Wade's army by retiring on hidden ways through the bogs. This hill has been painted by more artists possibly than any other Deeside landscape. It also contained two Lochs of justly renowned beauty, Kinnord and Davon, on which when we were small the head keeper's youngest son Johnny Mutch used to take us fishing. Having trawled with rod and line we would, before retiring, recork empty champagne bottles binding the neck with varying lengths of weighted line that ended in stout hooks baited with cheese paste. We left them to float overnight like lobster-pots in carefully selected places known to Johnny as the haunts of pike. Early next day we would return and with luck there would be several bottles zooming around at speed. The fun would then start, chasing them in a rowing-boat and hauling up well-fed and belligerent pike — a hilarious and exciting pursuit.

Dess House

Maud and Walter Davidson in front of the Dess rock-garden

Some years on when as late teenagers we formed part of the house-party for the Aboyne Ball, Aylmer Tryon who was one of our number while walking up grouse on Culblean was told by Mutch senior that there was no future in trying to flight duck on Loch Kinnord. This fired Aylmer into proving Mutch was wrong. He organised Tim Hayward and me to go to the Loch with him straight from the ball in our tails, having put guns and wellies in the boot of his car before setting off for the dance. I bet no-one had tried to flight duck in white tie and tails; but we did and thanks to the tall reeds and excellent cover round the Loch we came home with six mallard and a prodigious cleaners' bill to follow! Dear old Mutch was delighted.

Over the years we have enjoyed a host of happy times at Dinnet, starting in Violet's schoolroom and graduating to grown-up life, valetted, ghillied and fed like fighting-cocks in large congenial parties of people who all knew and liked each other well. Uncle Malcolm was a kind and thoughtful host and early in the war when I snatched a few days inter-patrol leave from *Tuna* at Aboyne he organised an ad hoc day's rough shooting for me with Andy, Hervey Cochrane of Findrach, himself, and one other I cannot recall. Mutch, in his late seventies, had been recalled to replace his successor absent with the Fifty-First Highland Division and gave us a splendid day on the low ground with grouse, partridge, pheasant and duck off Loch Davon at the end of which Lieutenant St John, with his then statutory tip of 5/- for a by-day in his hot hand, was thanking him and asking after my old chum Johnny who I recalled had won a scholarship to the RAF College at Cranwell. Mutch told me he was fine and in Canada, helping to set up the Empire Air-Training Scheme there. Remembering our age difference and the RAF habit of heaping rank in huge dollops on their appointed officers, I cautiously remarked that he must be somewhere well up the promotion ladder by then, so what was he? "I dinna rightly ken, Mr Michael" Mutch replied, "but I think its something they call an Air Vice-Marshall". The lieutenant blushingly handed over his brace of hot half-crowns to the AVM's dad who gravely and courteously accepted them without batting a single silver whisker – just a faint, fond quizzical smile perhaps? That is what made the north east of Scotland such a super place to be in those days. Such an example of unwavering, mutual respect and understanding between all walks of life and a natural ability to do things right and enjoy the process – Class never crossed our unfettered minds in those happy times.

Sir Henry Brooke had at the turn of the century helped and advised the renowned Glasgow self-made millionaire Geordie Coats of Coats' Cotton on the purchase of the neighbouring Forest of Glentanar. Having been elevated to the Peerage, Geordie styled himself the First Baron of that Ilk and proceeded to enjoy his new status as a laird of considerable consequence. He had notched himself a step or two up the social ladder by marrying Margaret Wellesley, a relative of the Duke of Wellington and, despite her patrician ways always known as Maggie, whom I mentioned among the surviving Aboyne denizens. They had one son, Tom, who in my time was reigning in his late father's stead. Tales about the ebullient and spherical Geordie are legion. As I have related earlier, both he and later Tom were great benefactors, building and endowing the beautiful silver granite episcopal Church of St Thomas's as well as a lion's share of the Victory Hall in Aboyne amongst other donations.

Geordie consulted Sir Henry about arrangements for his first big day on the grouse moor and was advised to invite all the neighbouring lairds whose estates marched with his. It was a little later that Sir Henry remembered that their number included one who was so notoriously dangerous that he had long since been struck off everyone's list to avoid further bloodshed and the total walkout of keepers and beaters. Horrified at his unaccountable oversight he rushed over to warn Geordie, but was too late to prevent an invitation being sent, so Geordie sent a telegram cancelling it on some pretext, the telephone not having reached the depths of the Grampians by then. Cleft-stick would be a more accurate description of this missive than telegram since it involved a boy bicycling four or five miles to the Aboyne post-office where it was duly registered and passed on to another mounted lad who set off the six or more miles to the addressee's mansion. In the process it failed to arrive in time to stop Dangerman setting forth; naturally his arrival caused a notable stir and a very red face for poor Geordie. However, he put him in the next butt to himself, in this case one from the top as Geordie like a good host had put himself in the top one. I suppose everyone knows the importance of keeping quiet on a grouse moor, where sound carries freely and the birds are wild and shy, so my readers will appreciate the sensation caused by what ensued. Roly-poly Geordie, having panted up the line chatting amiably to his guests turned at the top and proudly surveying the scene in a proprietorial manner shouted at the top of his powerful voice, "Here I am at last on ma twa feet – me and a' ma MILLIONS!!" Coveys rose in clouds off the beat not to be seen again that day.

Worse was to follow. Geordie, like most lairds, was provided by his keeper with a spaniel and equally like most lairds was unable to control it. The drive started and in due course those birds who must have been hard of hearing or making their own distinctive noises at the moment of Geordie's outburst arrived over the butts. Bang-bang, and off went the dog, lead, anchor and all with the kilted Geordie in hot pursuit and a flow of rich Gorbals invective. As he caught the offender and started to apply vigorous correction another covey came over. Bang-bang – you've guessed it. A right and left of number six shot slap up the kilted Geordie's obverse aspect. The wounded laird in righteous rage and some pain shouted "Ye've shot me ye bluidy fool and I wired ye not to come!" Dangerman departed and was never seen again on Geordie's forest or any other Deeside shoot either.

Tom Glentanar continued his father's philanthropy in many ways; he saw to the planting of trees in and maintenance of the beautiful Churchyard of St Thomas's. Being very fond of music, he also equipped the Church with a Baird organ of some consequence and an organist, Ian White, equally of some consequence who later helped to found and become the first Principal Conductor of the Scottish Symphony Orchestra. The church has become a regular feature for the many coach tours that now infest Deeside. Tom produced amateur opera with moderate success on the stage of the Victory Hall and built on to Glentanar Lodge a vast music-room complete with another (larger) Baird organ backing a fully equipped stage, plus two Steinway concert grands on a daïs in a wide bay window designed to accommodate them. It had a high, steeply pitched roof which was pine-clad and entirely lined with antlers that must have been both very dusty and acoustically disastrous.

Tom subsequently presented this organ to the Temple Church in London to replace the one they lost in the Blitz, and it is there to this day. Roger remembers being taken by Gan-Gan to Tom's inaugural concert on the opening of the new hall, for which he had engaged the Scottish Symphony Orchestra all the way from Glasgow and none other than the world famous Marcel Dupré from Nôtre Dame in Paris to play his new organ. It started with both orchestra and organ performing the Overture to the Meistersingers under the baton of Tom himself, by the end of which Roger swears Tom was at least two bars behind the players and the reverberations had sent several sets of antlers crashing down. Luckily no-one was hurt.

Later on another and subsequently renowned musical centre was established at Haddo Hall, seat of the First Marquis of Aberdeen and Tamair, the erstwhile Viceroy of both India and Ireland and one of the leading statesmen of his day, and his more than ample Marchioness Ishbel. She was much into good works, but also often with the overbearing manner she evidently acquired in her vice-regal days. She was far from beautiful as well as being vast so it caused the county great merriment when the Aberdeen Press and Journal, in reporting on an eightieth birthday tea-party given to her by the inmates of the nurse's rest home she had founded, got their descriptions of her attire and the birthday cake muddled. The resulting misprint read: "Lady Aberdeen was arrayed in 80 glacé cherries marking each year of her life, there being insufficient room for that many candles."

Old Aberdeen was another good-looking scion of the Clan Gordon; by contrast a smallish, spritely figure with a somewhat untidy, grizzled beard and a perpetual forward-bending posture as if about to execute a courtier's bow and resembling to my mind an Edward Lear drawing. He was on the stage of the Victory Hall one day in his kilt, together with Gan-Gan, as prominent members of the Deeside Society at their annual meeting. She had taken Roger along who tells me that from his seat in the body of the hall he was able to observe that the ex-Viceroy was clearly more practised in wearing ceremonial morning-dress than Highland regalia. There he was, seated legs apart with his kilt riding high over his knees unconsciously revealing to the assembled conservationists the full

My future wife! Craigievar, 1935. James, Pamela and Ivan Guinness

extent of his most noble endowments. Roger got so hysterical that he was removed to Bella Crichton's flat where she fed him endless drop-scones and goodies till the meeting broke up – a Godsend for him as you can imagine how bored a prep-school boy would be listening to all that conservationist bang-on.

One of the Haddo neighbours at Coull was a retired colonel of the HLI, Willie Lilburn and his wife Maud whose two sons, Alistair and Hugh, were our contemporaries. Willie was a twinkling sort of man of great energy and humour, despite having been seriously wounded, and he ran Coull with great skill – a bit of a hill farming and the odd grouse, exemplary forestry at which he had become an expert as was he also at bee-keeping and rearing Large White pigs. His heather honey, carried on to this day by Alistair, is known far and wide for its high quality. He had on one occasion found himself the recipient of Ishbel's hauteur, a border dispute or something like, and he held no love for her. Knowing that as usual she would be presenting the prizes at the important annual Tarland Show and 100% confident of winning the Sow-in-Litter class, he entered his prize Large White as "Ishbel of Coull". Revenge was sweet but Willie got cold feet and sent his pigman to collect the cup.

Another remarkable landowner in the Tarland district was the widowed Lady MacRobert; she also had sons our age – Alasdair, who had succeeded his father as the Bart; Roderick and Hughie. She had become a formidable power in the agricultural world, winning prizes at all the big shows, setting up the first prize herd of thorough-bred Aberdeen-Angus on her estate Douneside, building the first grain silos to be seen up there and much else besides, all her own efforts. A small, busy Scots person always seen dressed for town rather than for farming and wearing pince-nez. Tragedy unbelievable struck her early in the war for first Alasdair, then Roderick and finally Hughie in quick succession were killed fighting in the RAF. Typically Lady MacRobert gave Douneside, with a suitable endowment, to the RAF as a convalescent home for wounded personnel, renaming it 'Adastral House', and she single-handedly paid for a Spitfire that she had christened 'MacRoberts's Reply' – a really brave Aberdonian.

Five miles the other way down-river from Aboyne just short of

Kincardine-O'Neil you came to Dess, home of our very great friends the Davidsons. In the mid-nineteenth century the family had built a fine granite mansion on a hillside overlooking a bend of the Dee just below Drumnagesk, with superb views to the south and west over the forests of Birse and Glentanar and beyond the Ballater Pass to Loch-na-Gar. The family being capable architects as well as landscape gardeners, spotted this unique position and bought it, having waited a while to watch where the cattle stood in rough weather. There they built their splendid home growing out of the granite hillside and melting away into a beautiful rock garden — a perfect setting. At the same time they planted the grounds liberally and expertly with broad-leafed trees and beech hedges which, by my time, had formed a parkland of outstanding quality sloping down towards the Dee.

Frank and Nell were dear friends indeed, as were Frank's single brother and sister, Walter and Maud, kind, gentle people with great good humour and unbounded generosity. Nell was the gardener in our day and such was her skill that news of the Dess rock garden that she had created soon reached Balmoral and the acquisitive attention of Queen Mary. Queen Mary immediately invited herself to tea as was her wont when on the scrounge. Unlike Great Uncle Jim Thursby-Pelham with his antique furniture, poor Nell had no recourse to any subterfuge, short of digging up the whole lay-out and the Royal Daimler was duly bowed off laden with precious specimen rock-plants. Her Majesty only had to point her parasol at the object of her desire for it to be humbly offered and graciously accepted — she was an old devil that way and there was no escape for Nell.

My father was a skilled and well-known fisherman on the Dee and my parents often visited Dess in the Spring for him to go after the salmon on the Dess beat, then one of the better stretches of the river. Later in the autumn the Davidsons would ask Roger and me to try our luck with the autumn run and it was here I learnt to fish with a greased line and where at the age of 15 in the Long Haugh I landed my first fish — appropriately 15lbs "if a little on the red side". My father who was fishing below me had instructed the under-ghillie looking after me to let him know the moment I got into a fish and was soon on the spot. As I was wading far out and in swift deep water he shouted at me to turn my back on the river with the rod over my shoulder and thumb on the reel and come ashore; thereafter it was quite a party up and down the shingle for 20 minutes or so till judging the fish ready for the coup-de-grâce he told me to hold on, pointing the butt of my rod towards the salmon and walk back slowly. This I duly did, but as my father had misjudged how much line I still had out, I was off the shingle, up the bank, across the riverside path and over a barbed-wire fence into a fieldful of inquisitive bullocks before my fish came to hand. I could only just see the successful gaffing of my trophy, but I'll never forget the thrill of seeing my first fish – or Johnny Johnston the ghillie's well-mannered amusement for that matter.

Frank Davidson died later in the '30s and since there were no children, Dess passed to Maud and Walter, and Nell tactfully moved south – to Midhurst as it turned out – where my parents continued visiting her. My mother in particular shared many happy gardening occasions with her both at Dess and in the south, and like all good amateurs they swopped plants in profusion over the years. In fact it was half the charm of being taken round her garden by my mother that most of the plants and shrubs were identified as; "I got that from so-and-so" or naughtily "I nipped over the fence of a house for sale and got a cutting to produce that." After Great-Uncle Charlie died and Dorothy sold Craiglarach, she and her ex-German POW jobbing gardener dug up and transported a dwarf *Rhododendron praecox* that she had always admired in full bloom all of two miles over the bridge in a wheelbarrow – and with complete green-fingered success. Nell was likewise such a jackdaw or, as I term it, sponge-bag gardener and when she died she bequeathed her considerable collection of gardening books to my mother.

Maud and Walter continued the Dess tradition of kindness and hospitality. They were both notably ugly, but bursting with charm, humour and sagacity. Walter was a spry gnome-like person with a straggly moustache beneath his sharp, pointed nose on which perched his thick rimless spectacles and from the red tip of which a dew drop was forever threatening to fall. He was terribly short-sighted and so always peered through slitted eyelids, head thrust forward and with an unfailing, broad smile.

Maud's eyesight was equally poor and she favoured pebble pince-nez on her edition of the prominent family conk. A bustling, brisk person she was, shrewd and amusing, who ran the household with capability. She had a somewhat abrupt manner of speaking and her utterances were always matter of fact and concise. She told a delightful story that well illustrates the long forgotten days of contented domestic life in the big houses. It concerned their long-serving parlour-maid, Bella, whose increasing age had reached the point when the work at Dess was getting too much for her. With diplomatic skill and copious pains Maud suggested that Bella came to the rescue of dear old Colonel and Mrs So-and-so of a nearby much smaller establishment who were desperate for a parlour-maid. Bella was duly talked into coming to this rescue, albeit not without extended argument and a ration of ill-humour. But off she went, and a week or two later the Colonel and his lady had Maud and Walter over for Sunday luncheon – beautifully served in dead silence by a rather thunderous-looking Bella. Her hostess assured Maud that Bella was perfectly happy, found the work well within her limits and the house comfy and friendly and they were delighted to have her in their modest ménage. After lunch Maud asked if she might go beyond the green-baize door to have a word with Bella. No trouble, so once in the pantry Maud made searching enquiries to establish the cause of Bella's figure de bottine in the dining room. All was fine said Bella in reply to a succession of queries, but finally she admitted "It's nae the same, Miss Maud". Maud was furious and observed that it being not the same had been the whole object of the exercise, so what was wrong with that? The baffling reply revealing the underlying discontent was "They have rings in the room, Miss Maud!" Maud was utterly thrown by this surprising statement and retired to work out its meaning. Some time later they hit on the answer. Dess, like all houses of similar consequence, had its own fully staffed laundry so there were clean damask napkins for every meal – at the Colonel's you had silver napkin-rings.

A mile or so down-river from Dess lies Kincardine-O'Neil, straggling and winding for half a mile either side of the main road, in whose piscy church the Farquhars (and the four St John boys) had worshipped and where many of them, including my grandmother, lie buried. She played the organ for many years and when she retired the congregation presented her with a silver teapot heavily inscribed with their appreciation. Years later when his four nephews and only niece were dividing the Bletsoe spoils left to them by Andy, this unwanted article was sent for sale at Milne's Auction Rooms in Aberdeen where alas a Kincardine worthy spotted it and raised such hell that my cousin Oliver, my eldest Uncle Edmund's son and thus head off our sept, was compelled to buy it.

At the far end of this village stand the imposing wrought-iron gates of another mansion, Kincardine House, home of the Pickering family which soon became the property of yet another outstanding character, the eldest daughter Ursula Vaughan-Lee. She had also grown up with my father and uncles and was a close and valued friend. She had lost her husband in the First World War and never remarried, being more than content I fancy to bring up her two daughters (our contemporaries) and run her estate with unflagging efficiency. She was a good shot and we used to have great fun days with her after partridges and pheasants over her farms; and she was also a superb fisherwoman – probably the best lady rod of her day. She could not have been much over five feet tall (and Vaughan-Lee must have been tiny too for she always wore his plus-four suits when fishing or shooting), but she was built of granite, broad, sturdy, with round shoulders and head thrust forward, her thick grey hair brushed straight back and cut short. She possessed a pair of twinkling eyes, a bass voice, was perpetually smoking and useful with the Drams, and seemed the epitome of the outdoor person. She had a yen for fast cars and at one time owned a Bristol $3\frac{1}{2}$ litre sports saloon which even in old age she drove at prodigious speeds all over the county, miraculously without harm to life or limb. It was a memorable experience to see this Bristol careering towards you apparently radio-controlled and driverless, for all you could see from without was a waft of cigarette smoke and the odd stray lock of hair, Ursula's nose scarcely reaching as high as the boss of the steering-wheel. I can see her now at Craigveigh after my father's funeral, in tweeds relaxed in an easy chair with her short legs straight out in front and a goblet of strong whisky in her grasp, while holding forth on how it was "unfair of Tudor to go off like that – after all he's younger than me and now I have no-one to share jokes with". She was by a couple of years the elder and she survived another ten years well into her nineties, furious at the end that they had at last stopped her wading in the Kincardine water, one of the swifter and more dangerous stretches of the Dee. Those two were very close all their lives, chiefly I suppose because of their shared love of fishing, gossip and vulgar (but witty) stories – proper cronies you could say.

Continuing eastwards down the Dee, past the picturesque granite bridge of Potarch, you come to what was then the prime salmon beat, Cairnton, part of the Glassel Estate owned by the acknowledged father of greased fly fishing, Arthur Wood, whose book on the subject remains the bible for salmon-fishers. He was also a noted bee-keeper and it was fascinating for a schoolboy to be allowed to see the glass-fronted hives in his apiary. He had created round the house what must have been one of, if not the, largest rock garden, stretching out of sight in all directions and though striking not as beautiful as Nell Davidson's skilfully landscaped lay-out at Dess. Best of all though, were the labradors he bred and trained with endless love and patience. We were often taken to lunch at Glassel and I remember five of them round the dining-room, each lying down motionless under a console or serving table during our meal. This completed, the butler brought a large tray bearing five dogs' dinners to Arthur, who proceeded to call up each dog in turn, which came at once to sit beside him and was given a bowl of dog's dinner to hold in its mouth. It was then told to take the bowl to so-and-so, another dog. After performing this duty dog number one returned to lie down in its appointed place while the dog with its dinner before it did not move a muscle. This process was repeated, all five dogs in turn being called up to give a dinner to another, until all five were back under their tables, ears pricked, limpid dark-brown eyes fixed on Master. Arthur then gave the signal and instantly they were up and at it, the dinners gone in a matter of seconds, after which they retired quietly via the serving door. It was a sensational exhibition of dog-training and I reckon Arthur Wood could have taught Barbara Woodhouse a great deal. I am not sure whether he was divorced or a widower, but there was no Mrs Wood in evidence and he was most ably looked after by his charming secretary-cum-factotum Nancy Robinson, very popular and much sought after as an energetic and effective serving member of many of the local charity and/or social committees. Alas, when Arthur died the county, including I regret many Farquhars, about-faced and ostracised her as having been his mistress, driving her away from her native Deeside for ever. What appalling and cruel hypocrisy, "Let him who is without sin cast the first stone".

Further east beyond the small town of Banchory, you come to Crathes Castle seat of the Burnett's of Leys, then still very much in the possession of Jim and Sybil Burnett, the reigning Baronet and his beautiful wife. To Sybil in particular can be awarded the credit for recovering and re-instituting the Crathes gardens with such success that to this day they remain one of the principal attractions of the North East and a valuable study for both horticulturists and landscape architects — high immemorial yew hedges, authentic parterres, specie roses and above all Sybil's own particular white border, then one of the first of its kind. Jim was an important figure in Aberdeenshire, a retired Major-General, gregarious and widely popular, but a very stern overpowering father to his three children (once again our ages): Sandy his heir; Jamie and the stunning Titian-haired Rohays with whom, amongst a host of others, Roger at age 18 or so ran around with a good deal. Like the MacRoberts of Douneside the Burnetts faced great sadness in due course. First Sandy shortly before the war, fearful of failing his Mods at Oxford and the resulting onslaught from his father, committed suicide; and Jamie went to war with the Scots Guards and was killed before he was twenty — as usual a tragic waste of two charming people.

Eventually Rohays married a cavalry officer called Henry Cecil, younger brother of Lord Amherst of Hackney — a wild enough young man in all conscience who is reputed to have torn off one of a visiting General's medals remarking that he hated odd numbers — I can't think this is really true, but it is funny. Anyway, after siring three equally wild boys, he too was sadly killed. Jim Burnett died, one thinks, of a broken heart and after Sybil had gallantly kept the Crathes Estate going for several years with its historic and huge castle, gardens and many acres, it eventually ended up in the safe and capable hands of the National Trust for Scotland. Rohay's eldest son, Strongbow (of all unlikely names) changed his name by deed poll to Burnett, dropped Strongbow for Jamie and took over his grandfather's position through his mother as Burnett of Leys. He is now the incumbent of Crathes and helping to run the estate.

The younger two, David and Henry, are twins. In their salad days they were wont to set Deeside alight. One merry jape of theirs at a party with the young Caithnesses in the factor's house at Balmoral was to pinch the ignition keys from the cars of the Queen's dinner guests parked in front of the castle (including Roddie and Gabrielle Caithness who were on duty) and throw them away – We were most emphatically not amused – and the County enjoyed a plethora of blazing indignation and damnation of 'The Young'. Rohays was eventually remarried to the widower Cecil Boyd-Rochefort, the Queen's trainer and (as you may have guessed) the wild twins became the outstandingly successful team of horse coper (David) and trainer (Henry).

Across the river from Crathes lies the Durris Estate, which my father's crony Harry Baird inherited about this time. It had for many years been his family's home, but per se the house was a doubtful privilege since it is a ranging, gloomy, mid-Victorian pile surrounded by dark, moss-ridden lawns that fade into Stygian groves of laurel, monkey-puzzle and brooding cedars. Soon after interring his late mother Harry, having enjoyed a well-lubricated Sunday lunch, sallied forth into the autumnal wind and rain armed with a 14lb sledge hammer with which he demolished the outcrop of mini-tombstones she had erected under the cedars to mark the graves of a succession of ill-tempered pug-dogs. With this task zealously completed, he returned to his warm study fire-side, gave himself another goodly slug of celebratory malt and waited for oblivion to set in. Instead he was visited by the muse and composed the following *Epitaph to a Deceased Retriever*:

> "Beneath this lonely plot of ground
> Lies Pluto, useless sporting hound.
> The only things that he would hunt
> Were butcher's cart and bitches' ____.
> All day he'd lie upon the rug

Before the fire all warm and snug
And now he's dead he lies much snugger
The dirty, useless, farting bugger!"

So pleased was he with this creation that he forthwith phoned my father and recited it to him with two lady telephone operators listening in. You will rightly conclude from this episode that Harry Baird was an eccentric fellow and much of a law unto himself.

Scarcely five miles further east from Crathes you will find another large castle called Drum, fully able to compete with Crathes in historic interest and antiquity and the ancient seat of the Irvines with whom we also played around. Quentin, the heir, came to my daughter Hermione's rescue years later when she was rudely challenged as a St John for wearing her great-grandmother's Farquhar Tartan sash at the Aboyne Ball by the American (second) wife of Ian Farquharson of Invercauld. Quentin told her sharply she should know better than to challenge a St John on Deeside on that score and she retired suitably chastened. Incidentally she was the woman who when wading up to her waist in the Dee spotted the Queen Mother on the far Birk-Hall bank and was so overcome by the usual Royal smile and wave that she curtsied and was gaffed by her ghillie several hundreds yards further down at the foot of the pool. Gabrielle Caithness told us this story as she had heard it from the Queen Mother herself who confessed she had strolled down before tea with the idea of putting a worm through that pool – a heinous offence even in the autumn for it usually clears the water of salmon in a trice – and spotting Mrs Farquharson had quietly dropped her rod and tin of worms in the grass and made as if she was out for a stroll.

And now I turn north towards Alford and Donside, past Skene and Dunecht, Annie Cowdray's great house where the family sometimes competed to see who could ride her silver bicycle furthest into the lake and where she gave her famous tea-dances, sitting behind enormous silver tea-pots endlessly pouring the tea herself for the entire county.

Not far to the north is Monymusk, another historic estate belonging to the Grants who are the oldest Scottish baronetcy. Archie Grant reigned in those days and like Jim Burnett he led his family a hellish dance of discipline and deprivation which his long-suffering and utterly charming wife Evie bore with fortitude as did our playmates, his quiverful of sons and daughters. The youngest daughter, Christian, has written a delightful book about her childhood at Monymusk, illustrated with her own pen and ink sketches. The sisters were all attractive and full of fun and we enjoyed our parties with them greatly – particularly the dances. This was another house destined to lose its heir, for Arthur, the eldest, was also killed with the Scots Guards and his brother Francis succeeded to the title.

Now to the oldest and most picturesque of all the local castles, though by no means the biggest, Craigevar. Set to advantage on high ground overlooking the Leochel burn five miles south of Alford it is a fortified keep rising straight from the dungeons (then the kitchens) and capped like an Edmund Dulac fairy castle with pepper-pot turrets and a square balustraded tower bearing the banner of the Clan Forbes. It was the fortified seat of one of the numerous branches of that Clan who had attained a Barony and become Forbes-Sempill. In those days it was Jock and the stately Gwendoline who reigned with their son Billy the Master of Sempill, well known as a member of Alan Cobham's Flying Circus, and two daughters (more of our playmates): Margaret (Peggy), Roger's contemporary who later took to motor-racing and sadly died after sustaining long-lasting brain damage from an accident; and Elizabeth (Betty) who was a year or two older than me. We often stayed with them at Craigevar where I remember wild games round the policies and being taught by Betty how to make cigarettes out of lichen from the birch trees rolled in Bromo. She was afraid of thunder and I remember her rushing in and jumping into Roger's bed in the room I shared with him during a particularly bad storm. It could be frightening there to susceptible imaginations, for the castle and its grounds boasted a good supply of ghosts: a white lady disappearing up the stairs into the panelling in the Queen's bedroom; and a full-scale battle in the adjoining woods between the Forbes's and their enemies.

Thus it turns out that Roger shared his bed with, and I learned to smoke from, a girl who having grown up and qualified as a doctor at Aberdeen University turned into a man. As a girl she was not unattractive and danced superbly, especially Highland dances appearing in doublet and jabot over her dress kilt and topped by a well Brylcreamed Eton crop. Most boys, us included, were quite taken with her so it was a shock to one and all when the news broke. It also came as a nasty shock for the Forbes-Sempill family for having restyled herself the Honourable Euan Forbes-Sempill she claimed successfully from her kinsman the Baronetcy that went with her brother's title, understandably a far from popular move with the rest of the Clan. Sir Euan married his housekeeper in Alford where he was practising as a GP. It was odd anyway but in the Highlands it caused more than a sensation. Cecilia Sempill, Billie's wife, told us she had a spot of bother with her daughters at school (at North Foreland Lodge I think, the headmistress of which was another native of Deeside and ex-dancing partner of my youth, Fenella Gammel). They had just returned from the summer holidays and the form mistress was going round her class asking each girl to describe "the most exciting thing that happened to me last hols" when she came to the first Sempill child who exclaimed with great pride "Our aunt turned into an uncle" whereupon the mistress decided it was time for a game of rounders. The *Press and Journal* as usual excelled itself reporting their interview with the good doctor under the following headline and an appalling photograph: "'I'm yin 'o the Fechting Forbes' 'o' Craigevar' says Dr Euan."

Craigevar acquired quite different and fond associations for me and my family as Arthur and Patience Guinness took the castle for the grouse shooting (on the Craig Castle Estate) for three years running from 1935. They and their house guests, most if not all of whom we knew well, added a tremendous zest to the Deeside season. Pam and her brothers, aged 11, ten and nine, ran wild round the policies and had a marvellous time with the under-keeper ferretting and so forth. I alas was only there in '35 as thereafter I was off to China till war broke out, but Roger and my parents saw a lot of them up there.

A little way up Donside is yet another castle, Glenkindie, seat of the Forbes-Leiths which I visited frequently when loading for my grouse-shooting elders with Mary and Charlie Scott from America, the regular summer tenants. Charlie was English and the epitome of the fashionable Edwardian clubman and Mary his wife equally a typical example of the Bostonian upper-crust. They were generous and popular hosts and the shooting was excellent – I loved going there because we always arrived for a well-spread breakfast before setting out and Charlie often tipped me a fiver (a huge sum then and those beautiful white notes) on my last appearance.

Continuing up the Don you pass Candacraig, home of the banking Wallaces. Dandy Wallace who reigned in our day was an even bigger noise in forestry than Willie Lilburn of Coull. Then came more Forbes of Newe (to rhyme with Miaow). Sir John duly married Agnes Farquharson, the girl next door at Allargue, beside the Lecht Pass and Cock Bridge, and daughter of the Sunday lunch victims of Great-Aunt Dorothy's parsimonious catering.

I have followed my memory up and down the Dee and finally up the Don, touching on those people who recall something special, or possessed unusual or outré qualities. Allow my memory now to take me back from Cock Bridge, across the headwaters of the Avon (pronounced Arne) and the Royal Grouse Moors back to the Dee at Balmoral, crossing over by the castle to the south-side of the river past Birk-Hall and the Coyles of Muick, Dinnet and Glentanar to Aboyne, one of the most beautiful drives to be found in the whole world no matter the weather or the time of year – except of course when roads become impassable in winter snow!

Many other names are there – families taking part in all our activities and good friends for ever. Their names seem to weave a poetic spell over me as I recall the pleasure I had from their company. The Lumsdens of Pitcaple, the Hamiltons of Skene, the Forbes of Brux and of Corse, the Nicols of Ballogie, the Cochranes of Findrach and of nearby Balfour, the Coxs of Inchmalo, Davidsons in profusion at Dess, Minarloch and Alt-Dinnie. They and many others besides played and sang the summer through with us. Finally I come to what for me and many others was the highlight of the Scottish season, the grouse-shooting which like the golf deserves a chapter to itself.

Keith Caldwell with my parents, 1952

CHAPTER XIV

Shooting

J ust as I sat down to write this chapter, I heard first-hand accounts of my family's recent activities on the Perthshire moors and far from feeling jealous of their splendid days and great enjoyment with walking-up and driven grouse in plenty, it served to focus and refresh my recollections of the many times I equally enjoyed this sport while I was young enough. Now alas I doubt I could make more than 100 yards through heather and no longer can I climb a hill to my butt – so memories it is for me, but luckily mine live like yesterday.

I started loading for my uncles, senior cousins and great-uncles when I was about 12 years old, and as they were Scots and I came free, I was in great demand. I was also well coached by Great-Uncle Arthur, my senior and most frequent client for he contrived to sponge more invitations to shoot than any other Farquhar. You had to be strong and durable to be his loader for he hated being separated from any of his gear and he was a great one for having lots of it. Two guns of course, two out-size leather cartridge bags holding 100 each, a shooting-stick, a spare woollie and a heavy mackintosh rolled up in a leather sling; all this I had to carry – even both cartridge bags all day – while Uncle Arthur was mounted on a pony from which elevation a stream of instructions and occasional invective proceeded – "Mind those barrels", "I think I'd better put on another woollie – (or take one off)" and so on, never offering to take anything aboard his patient and sure-footed transport in order I suppose to leave both hands free for holding on. Admirals, except for the odd Mountbatten freak, are usually not at home on horseback. Thus laden I cannot remember ever being under stress climbing the hill through often knee-deep heather; at that age one makes molehills out of mountains. Ah well.

I was not only being well-trained as a loader, but was learning all the etiquette, the safety and the basic skills that soon stood me in good stead when at the age of 15 or so I started shooting with my father's old Cogswell and Harrison gun. All the family shot well and some shot superbly and in those halcyon days of well-stocked moors and frequent shoots I am judging them on the highest standards. It was nothing to see two in front and two behind falling out of the coveys from end to end of the line, and as most of the guns enjoyed four or five days grouse-driving a week, often with bags of 200 or 300 brace, it was not so surprising I suppose.

I have already mentioned Glenkindie and the Charlie Scotts where we were frequent guests and I clearly recall the early morning drives over Tillypronie and Descry to join the house-party for those sumptuous castle breakfasts, particularly with Uncle Arthur who by this time had acquired an Austin 16 hp saloon and mercifully had become less alarming on the road. This car had what for Uncle Arthur was a useful gadget in the form of a long lever on the inside of the driver's door that let the window up and down with a thump in one motion. He was very bronchial and thus well practised in the seaman's art of spitting to windward (or into the drawing-room fire come to that – poor Aunt Eve) and all the way over on our dawn run this window would be thumping up and down as the Admiral launched repeated high-velocity salvoes through it presaged by a succession of 'hoicks' that would have done justice to a Chinese rickshaw coolie. His range was so remarkable that he once put up a covey of grouse still half asleep in the morning mist beside the road on Descry Moor. He was still shooting driven grouse when he was 80 but like so many good shots as they grow old, though effective enough, he had slowed down to the point where he was unaware that he was swinging through the line – even with sticks on the butt to prevent such dangers. It thus became my duty, tactfully prompted by Charlie Scott, to get in the way regardless of the ensuing fury. I usually had to spot the birds coming as well, so I was busy and imprecations flowed freely.

Nothing beats a day's grouse shooting: the smell of heather honey on the bracing air; the superb scenery; the skill of the head-keepers controlling 30 or more beaters and flankers; the wind singing in the gun barrels and the excitement of watching the white flags of the distant beaters waving faster as a covey was flushed. Then watching the birds approach, swinging round the shoulder of the hill, disappearing into dead ground perhaps, before suddenly exploding over the butts, swerving, climbing, sliding, dipping and disappearing again in a rushing, whirring flash. And it was wonderful to me when I wasn't busy loading for my gun to watch the other experts dealing so effortlessly it seemed with those sporting coveys.

Then there were the lunches, borne in hay-boxes by the pannier-ponies, which took the bag back to base, and served by chauffeurs and footmen even when we sat on heather in the open. Some shoots had damask covered tables and silver laid out in the keeper's cottage or a barn or hut specially kept for the purpose – again liveried footmen and butlers operated and the feast was Lucullan being ably dealt with by appetites tuned to concert pitch by the champagne air and the exercise.

I was always Uncle Andy's loader when he was invited (less frequently than Uncle Arthur) to shoot. He was very methodical in his approach to the business, counting his cartridges into his bags before setting out and back into his magazine when we got home – a laborious proceeding but, allied to his precise record of the birds he shot, it allowed him to assess his performance accurately in his game book – it was usually three, occasionally four, shots per bird. He went equipped with a number of cards ruled vertically and horizontally into four quarters and two large black-headed pins. With one he secured the card to the front of the butt while the other was plunged into the appropriate range and bearing from the centre of the card representing his butt of each bird as it was shot – involving a number of jabs if he did well with a covey. A lot of guns used this device and it greatly helped the pick-up after each drive – perhaps it is still done?

There were many other relations for whom I loaded less frequently, including Uncle Arthur's sons Tom and John Farquhar, Uncle Charlie's son Bobby (but never Uncle Charlie for some reason) and most notably several times for cousin Keith Caldwell, the eldest Farquhar girl Kinty's son. He was a man of many talents being a linguist of note, brainy like his Cambridge don father, but above all a superb shot and zoologist of international repute. He was allegedly the finest grouse shot of his day and was consequently invited everywhere to the best shoots where he usually took John Keen, his own professional loader. It was only when the latter fell ill that Keith asked me to substitute, and this was truly a wonderful and demanding experience. I can remember in particular loading for him one day at Glentanar when amongst others in that superior line were the then Lord Aberdare, George Philippi and his wife (probably the best woman shot of her day); four of the finest performers then alive. It was of course on the best and most sporting beat, in fact *the* really big day, and the weather was superb. I have never seen the like of it again, they were so good and equally important, such pleasant company.

Keith was an enormous man with mighty weight-lifter's shoulders and torso matched by limbs like oak trees. Yet he moved more quickly and with neater economy of effort than most when taking a right and left in front and another behind, which he seldom failed to do if the birds were there. He was spectacularly ugly in a charming way, and had been from infancy causing unkind people to say it wasn't surprising poor Kinty died giving birth to him. Perhaps his greatest claim to fame was as one of the original white hunters in East Africa, in which capacity he took the Duke and Duchess of York on Safari in 1924. He later travelled widely as a Fellow of the Royal Zoological Society advising the Colonial Office on game preservation. He and his wife Kay lived in a charming house near Drumnagesk called Inneshewen where they threw large family get-togethers which, as you might suppose, always proved to be noisy and hilarious affairs with people of all ages swilling white ladies or drams. They were always kind to Roger and me and we were very fond of them, this being the reason why I have in this account of shooting in Aberdeenshire digressed in order to do them justice.

As a loader and later as a gun I have spent so many glorious days around that lovely country, Glenkindie, Descry, Tillypronie, Dinnet, Glentanar, Birse, Balfour, Ballogie, Findrach, Glen Dye, Glen Muick and so on – what a catalogue. What luck. Now, as I wrote at the start of this chapter, I can enjoy it all vicariously through my grandsons.

The Old Thatch

Pam and myself

Envoi

The enjoyment that I have had looking back to those good times and remembering that diverse collection of relations and friends with whom I shared them is so great that I cannot feel the slightest twinge of conscience at omitting all but occasional reference to the momentous progression of world events in the midst of which these goings-on took place.

That said though, I am aware that each succeeding generation claims in its time to have been a greater influence on the course of history than any other and I am no different. But this is no place to reiterate the catalogue of incredible changes that have taken place in my lifetime and those of my parents and grandparents, and anyway far abler writers than I have already done so and digressed on their consequences both good and alas too often evil.

It does, however, stagger me to think that two generations back from mine, Edmund St John was already five years old at the outbreak of the Crimean War while at about the same time Ellis Goodbody's uncles were starting to build the Midland Railway. My father characteristically defined the scope of his own lifetime by remarking, on the death of King George VI in 1952, that this would be the first funeral of a king or queen of England since William IV for which he would not himself have been on official duty.

In this bewildering acceleration in the pace of change it is for my parents' generation that I feel sympathy and admiration at the way they contrived to survive intact. Born and brought up in the heyday of Victoria's prosperous reign which free-wheeled them through to Edwardian indulgence, they were suddenly faced by the devastating impact of the collapse of the Courts of Europe in 1914 for which they were totally unprepared.

Theirs and my generation have of course since lived through two of the mightiest and most disastrous wars in the entire history of the human race, resulting in what I suppose future historians will describe as the greatest upheaval of old orders exceeding even those occasioned by the fall of Ancient Greece or the collapse of the Roman Empire.

And in between these twin Hells-on-Earth? Well can you blame us if in the '20s and '30s we were happy to make the best of it while we could and were inclined so to speak to fiddle while Stalin, Mussolini, Hitler et al were busy burning Rome? I freely confess (as you will have seen from this book) that for the most part that is what we did; but equally I feel free to say that I cannot conceive of how we could have prevented that 1939/46 repeat performance which ended so dramatically at Hiroshima and Nagasaki.

Not much remains of the people and places that I have written about: places as I remember them that is. Roger has several times been back to look at the Old Mill House at Benson which happily he says is as beautiful as ever and the adjacent cottages, that in our day were empty and dangerous ruins, have been salvaged and are now handsome and habitable once more. Unfortunately, it is now on the perimeter of RAF Benson, and the Thames is like a motorway with cabin cruisers. Southwood when I saw it some years ago was already carved up into separate flats. Hideous bungalows had been built all over my mother's beloved garden and the beech wood felled. Altogether a nightmare.

As for Deeside, the denizens have all gone, the villages expanded by soulless development following the advent of North Sea Oil. The buses even have followed the railway into oblivion and the Deeside road is a roaring procession of tourist coaches in the summer and skiers making for the Spittal in winter. Only a small remnant of the big houses are still in the hands of the families that once owned them, and above all not a single member of our branch of the Clan Farquhar remains there. For me that exceptionally beautiful stretch of country, which was such a well-loved part of my life, while still for the most part unspoilt is full of ghosts and I feel no urge to return.

Change is everywhere; change is perpetual. It is therefore better I think to remember and be thankful for the best of what has been and accept without regret that it will never be the same again. Dear old Henry Longhurst got it right when, writing in 1940 of his happy pre-war days as a golfing correspondent, which he then supposed were gone for ever, he entitled his book *It Was Good While It Lasted*.